CHURCH!

COME FORTH

The Preparation And Restoration Of Christians Raising The Dead

DIANE S. MORRISON

CHURCH! COME FORTH

As a point of clarification, when speaking of the global, corporate Church within this writing, I have taken the liberty to capitalize the word. When speaking of a specific local body or the building in which such a body meets, I have used the lower case form, "church." Similarly, when speaking of the corporate Body of Christ, I have capitalized that phrase, as well as the feminine pronoun "Her" when it is used to refer to that corporate Body as the Bride of Christ.

Cover design by Danny L. Martin and Aaron A. Stone

ISBN-10: 0-9743339-9-9
ISBN -13: 978-0-9743339-9-1
Library of Congress Control Number: 2006927837

Printed in the United States of America
Published in 2006

 **HERITAGE INK**

Marianna, Florida 32446
www.heritageink.com

DEDICATION

This book is dedicated to those individuals who determine to overcome the enemy of death in the earth. It is specifically dedicated to my family, especially my son, Drew, whom I prophetically declare to one day become a trumpeter of this message to his generation.

ACKNOWLEDGMENTS

My acknowledgments…

To the many individuals who initially contributed their knowledge and skills while I had to learn how to navigate through the unrelenting maze of decisions to find and settle upon the right beat and path of productivity pertaining to this message.

Specifically, to Tom and Drew for their input and enduring patience while the whole equilibrium of our home shifted as I spent countless hours writing and re-writing this ever unfolding message. Your patience merits reward that only God can give.

To Prophetess Jane Hamon of Christian International, Santa Rosa Beach, Florida, for unconditionally yielding her prophetic voice whereby the message of this book was called forth from conception into reality.

To Dr. Nancy Weidner of Weidner Chiropractic Clinic, in Menomonie, Wisconsin, for being that much needed confidant and sounding board in all aspects of this writing, for providing a conducive environment in which to write, and for being a primary motivator in seeing that this writing came to completion.

To Miss Laurie Skipper of Wichita, Kansas, who willingly and graciously offered her spiritual insights and technical skills while exercising patience as this message continued to unfold, and unfold, and unfold…

To Mrs. Sharon Miller of Heritage Ink, Marianna, Florida, for her corroboration, and patiently going the extra mile in helping me to work through my thinking on this subject, and the many resulting changes.

To Martha Lucia of The Watchman Network, Santa Rosa Beach, Florida, for an unfortgettable four and one-half hour meeting toward the end of this project, and which greatly contributed to the final shaping of this book. The "reformational" significance of this message was not realized until we met. The drive home that night was sobering. Thanks for being there for me when I need it.

To Bishop Bill Hamon of Christian International, Santa Rosa Beach, Florida, for approaching me and volunteering support by requesting to foreword this book. Your example and experience as a pioneer of new truth reflects an invaluable arsenal of Godly wisdom from which I'm bound to continuously reference while spreading this message. You blazed a trail that enabled me to discover another.

To most of all, the financially committed individuals and ministries who helped make it possible for me to be home in order to set aside more time to write. Admittedly, you are the backbone of what has been accomplished. Along this same line, a heartfelt and special thanks is in order to Mrs. Gay Owens in loving memory of her son, Mr. Bill Foran.

Contents

SECTION ONE
INDIVIDUAL AND PRACTICAL CONSIDERATIONS

SECTION TWO
CORPORATE AND THEOLOGICAL CONSIDERATIONS

CHURCH!
COME FORTH

COMMENDATIONS

See what others are saying about this book at:
www.churchcomeforth.com

FOREWORD

Every so often a book is produced that challenges the reader to go beyond normal Christianity. Diane writes with conviction and revelation about a subject that very few have dared to explore. She touches on a biblical principle that has been the passion of my heart for over 50 years of ministry. That is, the progressive restoration of truth back into the Body of Christ, the Church.

The beginning of the restoration of the Church started with the Protestant Movement. Martin Luther's revelational teaching of justification by faith was revolutionary and stirred great controversy among the established Christian leaders of that day. Diane's presentation concerning Christians believing for the faith to raise the dead will stir great controversy among some but will be welcomed by others, especially those who are sensing the same challenge.

Diane approaches the subject as God dealt with Israel through the prophet Isaiah, "Come and let us reason together." She does not present herself as an expert with all the answers or one who can fully manifest "raising the dead". To proclaim biblical truth we do not have to be able to fully demonstrate that truth in our personal life. It makes it more acceptable when the hearer can see it proven by a living demonstration; however, that does not change the reality of the truth.

Biblical truth is God's revealed will and eternal reality whether anyone is believing or demonstrating that truth. I have a right to preach God's power for victory over sin and divine healing for my body even if I am not living victorious over all sin and obtaining freedom from every sickness and affliction. All the reader has to determine is whether the material presented here is a biblical truth. If so, as a believer we should expect to raise the dead at times as well as speak in tongues, heal the sick and cast out devils.

The devil is the enemy of every Christian. Satan comes against us to rob, destroy and kill. His objective is to bring death to the spirit, soul and body of mankind, especially Christians. He seeks to kill the spirit with sin, the soul by convincing people not to practice God's principles, and the body with accidents, sickness and terminal diseases. All of these things are agents of the spirit of death. Jesus by His death, burial and resurrection overcame sin, sickness and death. Now "the law of the Spirit of life in Christ Jesus has made me free from the law of sin and death."

Each restoration of truth in Christ's Church has enabled believers to appropriate more of what Christ has provided for His children. The last truth restored will bring revelation and faith to overcome the last enemy. This will climax universally with the second coming of Christ. But at this time, God is challenging His people to increase their faith to raise up those who have had an untimely death. Diane thoroughly examines how we can determine whether a death is premature or in God's timing. The death of Lazarus was untimely so Jesus restored him back to life, but eventually his appointed time came to leave this earth through death.

Thanks, Diane, for receiving the vision and burden from Christ Jesus to make this challenge to the Body of Christ. This book could start a chain reaction causing thousands of Christians to demonstrate the Lordship of Christ over all things, including untimely deaths. God bless you for your willingness to participate in the persecution that comes with the presentation of new truth. As a pioneer of new truth, let me assure you that the opposition from unbelievers is not worthy to be compared with the joy and reward of seeing Christians becoming full believers demonstrating God's power and reaping the great harvest of souls.

Dr. Bill Hamon

Apostle/Bishop of Christian International Ministries Network (CIAN)

Author of:
The Day of the Saints
and 8 other major books

Preface

~

On December 9, 2001, an unexpected and life changing, prophetic word of the Lord was given to me from the speaker's platform during the middle of a Sunday morning service. It was one that would significantly alter the course of anyone's personal destiny who received such a word. A portion of this prophetic word was:

> "...the Lord says, just begin to write and He will begin to orchestrate the message that's going to come forth from you. God has already put it in your heart. Go ahead and write it, and the Lord says that He will deliver the message from throughout the four corners of the Earth."

Only God and close family members knew that this message had indeed been floating around in the recesses of my spirit for about three months before this prophetic word came forth. In fact, a few pages of notes had already been jotted down with the fleeting intent of teaching this material. Obviously, God had in mind another way of communicating this message.

The thought that this message would be sent throughout the four corners of the earth was staggering. It was one of those prophetic directives that could have easily been shelved, given the stated and far reaching impact. The directive, however, merited serious consideration in that it was delivered from a credible prophetess of God. After giving the prophetic word serious consideration, the gravity and responsibility of what would be required began to settle within my spirit.

I am unsure whether I staggered more at the thought of writing a book, or the idea of penning a message of this nature. It is an understatement to say that both directives were overwhelming. The notion of writing a book was never a serious consideration before receiving this prophetic word. Another small portion of this prophetic word, not previously shared, sealed the fact that I must move past my tentative mentality and author this text. In it, God told me, unequivocally, *not to argue with Him* regarding this directive because He had specifically put it in my heart to write this message.

Once I began to seriously entertain writing this message, I began to baulk for good reasons. First, the content of this material was, generally speaking, unconventional, socially questionable and potentially controversial. This is especially true in the western world from where this message would originate. If you are from a geographical region other than the western world where raising the dead is more common, it is important you take this western world perspective into consideration as you read this book. Evidently, it was God's desire for someone in the western world to write this message, as noted by the prophetic directive.

Second, I began to discover that research materials on how to raise the dead were neither abundant nor readily available. Stories could be found about individuals who had been raised and their heavenly experiences while away from the earthly realm. However, finding stories where the elements of faith used to work the miracle of resurrection were pointed out and emphasized was virtually veiled. It became increasingly apparent that the orchestration of this message would indeed have to come directly from the Holy Spirit.

As if these issues were not enough, one more very important issue began to surface. Writing a book of this nature would surely create an expectation that I practice what I preach. An occasion to be personally involved in raising the dead had not yet presented itself. Obviously, thoughts concerning my spiritual destiny began to unfold in a more sobering manner at this point.

I came to grips with the fact that it was incumbent this message be written, regardless of any and all ongoing apprehensions, not to mention the lack of experience on my part. God had specifically directed me to write it, and there was no arguing. With this in mind, the simplicity of this writing and how it is received within the Body of Christ rests in God's Hands. I have simply done what I was prophetically directed to do.

I might add, now that I have the Word of God in me regarding this subject, and have had occassion to be directly involved in these experiences, the thought of entering into these situations is not so far removed from my will and spirit. Neither will it be for you once you allow the message of this book to saturate your mind and spirit. This message is about how the corporate Body of Christ can make natural preparation now to raise the dead in the event of a premature death, and why it is essential this resurrection miracle be restored to the Body of Christ before Jesus will return.

As you will see, much biblical education and spiritual fortification on this subject can be gleaned and assimilated long before someone dies. In fact, it would be to our advantage to enter in to these situations only after having made preparation in this regard. Faith for raising the dead will come by hearing what the Word of God has to say on this subject, NOW, long before anyone dies!

Despite the conventional thinking of unbelief surrounding deceased individuals being resurrected, faith-filled and governmental Christians are duty bound to mobilize for the purpose of raising the dead when it comes to the premature death of others! With this in mind, the objective of this book is to shed light on some fundamental insights concerning Christians raising the dead, as well as to offer the wisdom of some basic guidelines. Faith-filled believers will instinctively begin to better respond and react according to God's Word in varying situations of death as they allow this message to drop down into their spirits. Consideration for raising the dead will become as natural and common as the thought to pray for someone who is ill.

When believers begin taking an active show of interest to become biblically educated on the subject of how to raise the dead, momentum will be generated for educational platforms of development and maturity. The restoration of Christians raising the dead will once again become an integral part of Christianity. And, the earthly Church will begin taking one more step toward the ultimate fulfillment of Her earthly destiny. Her enemy of death will visibly begin to become the footstool of Jesus!

To this end, I say, *CHURCH! COME FORTH.*

INTRODUCTION

~

To quote a saying I once heard, *the writing of a subject is the learning of it*. Nothing could be closer to the truth regarding the subject of how Christians enter into the dimension of raising the dead. After all, who sits around and talks about Christians raising dead people? Not many people — yet. Perhaps this is because the phrase is many times associated with something scary or of a cultish nature that would make some shy away and dismiss the subject. This response may sound plausible to some, however, Christians who believe in the miracle-working power of God in this manner know otherwise.

These particular Christians know the dead can be raised in the name of Jesus Christ, even though the occurrences are seemingly few and far between. Rather than raising an eyebrow or dismissing the thought of a resurrection, it captures their attention. An in-depth understanding of raising the dead, however, has been somewhat skewed when it comes to seeing or hearing of someone who has been raised.

We have had a tendency to focus more on the person whose life was restored rather than the person who was responsible for seeing that the earthly resurrection came about.

It is so easy to get caught up in hearing about what a resurrected person experienced while out of their body and in the spirit realm that the tendency exist to subconsciously overlook what caused their life to be restored in the first place. As a result, an in-depth look at the dynamics that trigger such a miracle have usually gone unexplored. This oversight will have to change in order for the Body of Christ to further advance in this area. Our focus will have to shift to the faith-filled actions of the people ministering resurrection life.

One other possible reason that this subject has not been readily discussed has to do with the timing of God. Perhaps it has not been on God's progressive timetable for this subject to come to light in a corporate manner. Whether it has, or has not, now remains to be seen. Regardless of our varied opinions on this aspect of timing, the revelation of this subject is now being released and disseminated among the Body of Christ in corporate fashion.

Our understanding of this subject should initially be premised upon what the Scriptures of the Holy Bible have to say about this subject. In addition, there is nothing like real life experiences to complement what the Bible has to say about Christians raising the dead. Hopefully, we will take the opportunity in the future to capture pivotal words and actions of faith in theses situations with more revelation and insight under our belt. This will be necessary if we want to begin to see the dead raised, and raised on more than just an extremely rare basis.

If you have heard of someone being raised from the dead, reflect back on the story. Are you able to reflect back on what you heard and make any pertinent observations about the individuals who ministered to the deceased? Can you pinpoint certain actions of faith that ignited this outcome? Are there any recognizable spiritual keys that triggered such a result? At what pivotal point in the process did the relatives and/or ministers rise up and refuse to allow the deceased to remain in the spirit realm? What social barrier of unbelief, if any, did those ministering have to cross?

Questions such as these will be addressed in this text. However, before delving into the insights of these questions, a scriptural foundation should first be laid. The chapters in *Part One* will lay that foundation with the scriptural reasons for why we, as believers, should desire to raise the dead. Answers to the plethora of questions can then be more readily received once we foundationally understand why we should even approach this subject at all.

Once that foundation has been established in *Part One*, discussion of how to go ahead and start making preparation now to raise the dead is presented in *Part Two*. Do not think that raising the dead is so far removed from you that you could never be a part of such a miracle. We will see that this miracle is closer than we think.

Part Three discusses how we can and should expect raisings to begin happening. It will not be the predictable *business as usual* when someone prematurely dies, and believers in the Body of Christ begin to act upon this message. It goes without saying that frequent occurrences of this earthly miracle are in the destiny of the corporate Church.

We will also see in *Part Three* that when deceased individuals are raised, the Church will need to be prepared for salvation opportunities. Additionally, there are those individuals responsible to spearhead this dimension. Their job is to spread this message and demonstrate the manner of the kingdom of God in this regard so that this enemy called death is overcome in the earth and made the footstool of Jesus.

The last section, *Part Four*, partially reveals how what we are doing on an individual level translates into what God is doing on an overall corporate level. When we understand what God is doing on

Earth, within the Church, we can more readily recognize and better grasp old truths being restored to the Body of Christ on the subject matter at hand.

The overall message within this book may or may not be readily embraced. This may depend on your understanding of what God is doing in the earth and how He is using His saints to usher in His plans and purposes. On the other hand, you may very well embrace the truth of raising the dead in a whole new light and perspective, especially when someone close to you dies a premature death.

Whether you choose to embrace this message or not, it is between you and the Lord. Regardless, the Church has been in the dark on this subject long enough. Let's not stay there any longer. It is now time for the Church to come forth out of the darkness and unearth this subject!

PART ONE:

LAYING A FOUNDATION OF FAITH

The purpose of Part One of this text is to lay down a general foundation for discussing the subject of raising the dead. One of the first, essential building blocks addressed is that of removing the hindrances that prevent us from feeling like we cannot talk about this subject, especially if we have not experienced raising the dead. Additionally, old mind-sets and traditional ways of thinking that have prevented the Body of Christ from entering into this dimension will then be somewhat dispelled as well.

We will gradually see that discussion of these fundamental issues will greatly advance our efforts in clearing the path of this dimension so we can have the freedom and liberty to enter into death situations without hesitation.

CHAPTER ONE

~

LET'S TALK

ABOUT

RAISING THE DEAD

"Why should it be thought incredible by you that
God raises the dead?"

Acts 26:8

Responding to an occasion of death has been fairly predictable throughout history. Generally speaking, the loved ones left behind plan a funeral or memorial service and follow through with some type of burial or disposal of a body, given the fact that there are remains. This has long been the conventional response and manner in which individuals have responded. This response will gradually begin to change when we as Christians begin to realize the spiritual potential resident within us to start exercising our faith to raise the dead.

A further examination of this response is the starting point where Christian believers should begin to realize that we have no other choice but to begin crossing the thresholds of culture and convention if we are going to raise the dead. For example, we may still end up planning for a funeral. But somewhere in the midst of that process, an unconventional and active faith to intervene will spring into action, regardless of who is around and what might be taking place. This statement will make more sense as you continue reading.

Stories have increasingly been conveyed to me about individuals who were ministered over to be raised but were not. My insight and perception into the majority of these situations is that most of the ministry took place shortly after the person died. This is, of course, the most opportune time for us to exercise our faith, before our emotions overwhelm us and doubt has time to creep into our minds. However, it is not the only time available for us to minister. This is a fact we need to begin to realize, especially in light of the scriptural basis for so doing.

Some of the stories that have been shared with me involved praying inconspicuously or secretly in the funeral home parlor well ahead of the actual funeral service. In other words, ministry for the deceased usually took place early in the process. When that attempt was unsuccessful, no further act of faith was made to attempt to press in and see the restoration of that life.

We will have to examine this response, and others, if we, as believers in Jesus Christ, are going to successfully demonstrate the Kingdom of God in this manner. There is so much more that can be done on our part as well as on the part of other believers. As believers, we must prepare and educate ourselves accordingly. There are reasons why preparation and education are necessary.

One, we need to be prepared to deal with unbelief. *To be forewarned is to be forearmed.* At best, our actions are likely to be perceived as out-of-the-ordinary and, possibly, as incomprehensible to the unbelieving. When there is a pervasive spirit of unbelief, there is the likelihood that even the strongest of believers can be prevented from moving in the miraculous. Scripture tells us that Jesus, Himself, could do no mighty works in his hometown of Nazareth because of the unbelief that prevailed. We need to be prepared to stand in the face of such potential unbelief. This fact leads to the need for education.

Teaching on this subject is extremely vital in order for believers to realize that we, too, can learn how to exercise our faith to raise the dead. The place to begin learning is, of course, from God's written Word, the Bible. Scales will begin to fall from our eyes when we go to the Scriptures and begin observing, with an open mind, the behavioral insight and wisdom of the resurrection stories provided for us there.

Actions required to raise the dead can be considered out of the ordinary to an unbeliever. In fact, we will begin to see that these actions could sometimes be very offensive to some of those gathered around. Nevertheless, the idea is that we become more educated on this subject so we will know what we are doing in our pursuit to raise the dead. If we do not first allow what the Word of God has to say about raising the dead to saturate our mind and spirit, then we may perhaps allow the unbelief of others to prevent us from moving in this manner. Faith for raising the dead will begin to come, and will continue to come, by hearing what the Word of God has to say on this subject.

When truths from the Word of God on this subject truly begin to drop down in our spirit, the battle for another's life will not be as fruitless as in the past. We can learn how to battle and continue pressing in to this enemy of death when it knocks on our door. Should we find ourselves faced with a situation of premature death, the information and revelation contained within this text should provide sufficient wisdom and insight for the battle.

Is it any wonder that the Church has, for the most part, been ineffective up until this point where raising the dead is concerned? The Body of Christ basically has not known how to approach these situations. Hopefully, this will no longer be the case after reading this text. It will then be a matter of putting words into action when we are put to the test to intervene.

The overwhelming consensus at present is that intervening in these particular situations is much easier said than done when all factors are realistically taken into consideration. While this may be true, the biblical fact remains that believers *shall* raise the dead as a testament to the resurrection power of the Lord, Jesus Christ, for the glory of God. With this in mind, we have to start somewhere.

> When God starts to reveal what He wants to begin taking place in the earth, dialogue and discussion may abound long before the visible demonstration begins to unfold.

WHERE DO WE BEGIN?

Biblical grounds for raising the dead should be immovably solidified within the mind and spirit of every believer desiring to see the demonstration of the dead raised. In other words, what biblical right entitles believers within the Body of Christ to participate in this kind of activity? Who is initially responsible for initiating action with regard to raising the dead? A loved one? A minister? Or simply a believer who happens to be available at the time? How do we move into these situations? When do we consider a death as premature? Some potential answers to questions like these will be explored in this book, along with other related issues.

Educational materials addressing how believers in the Body of Christ operate in this dimension are not yet in abundance. However, a lack of published works should not be construed to mean that we are out of order in approaching this subject. When God starts to reveal what He wants to begin taking place in the earth, dialogue and discussion may abound long before the visible demonstration begins to unfold.

I like the saying, *Talk it 'til you walk it.* Stated another way, we will probably hear and read more about the topic of the dead being raised before we have the opportunity to experience seeing it happen. Hopefully, we will have had time for this type of spiritual information to drop down and absorb in our spirit through dialogue and discussion before we actually need to exercise it.

There is relatively little discussion of how believers go about raising the dead when compared to healing the sick or casting out demons. The subject of death carries within it a sense of finality that has unconsciously hindered believers from discussing this matter in depth. This fact will gradually begin to change as believers feel the liberty to discuss this subject at face value rather than needing to feel qualified to approach it. Thus, the first major barrier needing to be addressed is that of getting believers to talk about the subject.

LET'S TALK ABOUT RAISING THE DEAD

Skepticism, which is just a form of unbelief, emerges quickly in most of the new settings where I find myself discussing this subject. The most common question, inevitably asked almost immediately, is, *Have you ever raised the dead?* The skepticism is revealed by the tone and motive behind the question, rather than the question itself.

The underlying message in the tone of the posed question is that this subject cannot be credibly discussed unless we have raised the dead. This is a fallacy that must be addressed. When it comes to discussing the biblical truths of believers raising the dead, whether a person has actually raised someone from the dead or not is irrelevant. In order to address this fallacy head-on, let me pose my own question in response.

When is an appropriate time to discuss and talk about raising the dead? When someone dies? Nonsense! Do we wait until someone needs a miracle of healing in their body to find out what the Word of God says about healing? Or, do we wait until someone needs deliverance from demonic spirits before we search the Scriptures to see what God's Word says about that subject? The answer to both of these questions is, *absolutely not!*

As believers, we should have already equipped ourselves to deal with either of these situations. Otherwise, we are likely to come up short when we encounter either situation. Why should we handle the issue of raising the dead any differently? It is equally important to know what the Scriptures say on this topic. We should know how to pray for resurrection, just as we know how to pray for healing or how to cast out a demon.

Sadly, this subject is not usually discussed except when someone has died. This is the most inopportune time to start preparing and equipping ourselves to raise the dead. Our lack of preparedness has caused us to be highly ineffective in this area. Why wait to get ourselves prepared to raise the dead when we can prepare now? Now is the time to make preparation, not when someone dies.

We do not wait until we witness someone in cardiac distress with no pulse and no respiration to go take a course in CPR. As conscientious citizens, we take the course, gain the knowledge, and prepare ourselves — just in case we ever encounter such a situation and can be the instrument used to save a life. Likewise, we should not wait until we are faced with a death to begin preparing ourselves to be able to be the instrument used by God to restore a life. The time has come for the Body of Christ to go to the Word of God and start discussing the various aspects of this subject so that when someone dies a premature death we know we have another option.

As with the CPR analogy, we need to be prepared ahead of the crisis. We should be prepared and know what to do if we encounter a situation where there is a need for healing or deliverance. Raising the dead, in all reality, is no different from healing or deliverance. It takes the same faith. It may seem to take a greater measure of it, but it is still the same faith! If we have learned how to minister healing or deliverance to individuals, then it stands to reason that we should be able to learn how to minister resurrection life to them as well.

With this in mind, will believers ever learn how to go about raising the dead if we continue to, consciously or subconsciously, dismiss this subject on the basis of lack of experience? The answer to that question is, *probably not*. The need exists to talk now. Whether or not we have raised the dead is a totally irrelevant and spiritually shortsighted requirement. What *is* relevant is knowing what the Word of God has to say on this subject long before anyone dies. Our qualifications to do this are based on being a believer in Christ Jesus and nothing else.

For future reference, individuals questioning our desire to discuss this subject should be met with answers such as the following ones: *Even though I have not raised the dead yet, I want to know what the word of God has to say on the issue so that I can be prepared to do so when that is needed. No, I have not yet raised the dead, but I anticipate that the opportunity to do so will eventually present itself.*

These are just a couple of responses to keep in mind and consider if we find ourselves being challenged while talking about this subject. Tearing down this subtle barrier that says we cannot talk about raising the dead since we have not yet done so needs to be recognized for what it is. It is a lack of spiritual insight on this subject. The bottom line is that just because we have not raised the dead should in no way be construed to mean we are not qualified to do so, or to discuss the subject. To the contrary, we should all the more begin discussing this subject so we can learn how to go about raising the dead when the occasion presents itself.

Classrooms are full of people who have yet to experience what they may be doing in the future. Sure, these classrooms are ideally taught by experienced individuals. There has been a serious shortage of teachers within the Body of Christ who have raised the dead. For this reason alone, we should fully embrace, discuss and instigate dialogue regarding this dimension. It will only be a matter of time until teachers with experience begin to emerge on the scene. The Body of Christ will then be in a better position to discuss raising the dead from a platform of experience, and not just from revelation of the truth.

Until that time comes, truth is still truth, and should be taught.

THE TIME IS NOW

Remember, the most inopportune time to begin preparing to raise the dead is when someone dies. Why not prepare ourselves for the spiritual future as we would prepare for our natural future? Do it now! Know that we will have to ignore the many taboos that the majority of individuals associate with this subject in order to discuss it. We need to identify other believers who share our sentiment toward this subject. Discuss this subject with them and let's get our thoughts out into the open.

The scenario we should try to avoid is being thrust into a pressure cooker situation before we are ready to enter into this dimension. We should prepare ourselves so that we are ready when the time comes. With these thoughts in mind, let's start talking...

CHAPTER TWO

~

BIBLICAL RIGHT
OF RECOURSE

"Most assuredly, I say to you, he who believes in
Me, the works that I do he will do also; and greater
works than these he will do, because I go to My
Father."

John 14:12

    The ultimate power of death rests in the sovereignty of God.
Selah! Beyond this fact, however, is a God-given biblical right of
believers to raise the dead in the event a death has been deemed
premature. This right of recourse, which is one of the primary
premises upon which this book is biblically based, is best stated in
John 14 of the New Testament.

Jesus made a prophetic statement in John 14:12 that can be staggering to the human mind. He said, *"Most assuredly, I say to you, he who believes in Me, the works that I do he will do also; and greater works than these he will do, because I go to My Father."* This can be interpreted in two different ways. First, believers should do greater works because they would be around on the earth a lot longer than Jesus. Second, any work that Jesus did while He was on earth, He said that believers would be capable of doing greater. He knew times would grow more trying for believers. It is my belief that Jesus was alluding to both aspects in this directive when it comes to the power of God being demonstrated in the earth.

Jesus demonstrated the power of God when He healed all that were sick, cast demons out of people, turned water into wine, etc. As if these miracles were not enough, Jesus raised individuals from the dead. When we couple these facts with the statement Jesus made that believers would do greater than this, we question to whom He was referring.

WHAT IS A BELIEVER?

The word *believers* can be very ambiguous in that there are many different kinds of believers in Christ Jesus. To mention just a few, there are baby believers, immature believers, underdeveloped believers, uninformed believers, maturing believers and even false believers. All of these are people with whom we associate every day. Many of them believe *in* Jesus, but just what do they believe *about* Jesus? There are many others who believe *in* Jesus without ever becoming what we typically mean when we refer to *believers*.

For example, Muslims believe in Jesus. In fact, James 2:19 states, *"even the demons believe!"* So, not all who believe *in* Him are *believers of* who He really is. As Simon Peter so aptly stated in Matthew 16:16, Jesus is *"...the Christ, the Son of the living God."* As you can see, not all entities indentifying themselves as believers in Jesus Christ, the Son of the living God, may not invoke the power of the Holy Spirit to demonstrate the greater works Jesus said believers would do. Given this fact, just what kind of believer was Jesus alluding to when He made this statement in John 14:12?

A working definition of the word *believer* needs to be established for the sake of clarity. First and foremost, a *believer* is one who has repented to God of his sin and accepted Jesus Christ as his Lord and Savior, the only way in which to be reconciled to God the Father and entitled to live eternally with God (Father, Son and Holy Spirit) in heaven. *Believers* believe *in* Jesus Christ and the work that He did on the cross to bring about this reconciliation.

Further, it is the author's opinion that Jesus was alluding to those believers in Him who aspired to live a life on this earth which is reflective of His Word and ways. While maturing believers endeavor to walk in the Word and ways of God here on earth, there are other benefits associated with believing in Jesus Christ. These benefits have to do with the power of God. Several of these benefits are given in Mark 16:17-18.

> *[17]"And these signs will follow those who believe: In My name they will cast out demons; they will speak with new tongues;*
> *[18]they will take up serpents; and if they drink anything deadly, it will by no means hurt them; they will lay hands on the sick, and they will recover."*

According to this Scripture, we should be able to cast out demons and speak in tongues if we are a believer in Jesus Christ. If we go back to the original Greek text and also understand the Hebrew colloquialism being used in this passage, we find that we should be able to *take [on]* an evil person *(a snake)* or even Satan himself *(the Serpent)*, with the implication being that we do so successfully and victoriously. If we unknowingly drink something that is contaminated or toxic in some way, it will *by no means* harm us. We should also know how to lay hands on the sick and expect that they will recover.

In light of all this information, the majority of us still have some maturing to do when it comes to encountering individuals who are as mean as snakes or drinking a poisonous drink! I think it would be safe to conclude, in all honesty, that most believers would prefer to be speaking in tongues and laying hands on the sick rather than casting out demons or dealing with venomous people and poisonous issues.

Nevertheless, these various facets of ministry come with the territory of being a believer. But, they do not happen just because we say we are a believer. As a believer, each of us has the responsibility to give ourselves to the biblical word and ways of God in order to be able to minister in this given capacity. For the sake of distinction, I will use another term to pertain to those who will do greater works than Jesus. The term I have chosen for those believers is *Christian*.

WHAT IS A CHRISTIAN?

We can read in Acts 11:19-26, where ..."*a great number believed and turned to the Lord*" at the Antioch church. We can conclude from this verse that there are those who believe AND turn their ways to the Lord. On the other hand, there are those who believe and do not personally turn their ways over to the Lord. Barnabas and Saul were so encouraged by the great number of people at the Antioch church who believed AND turned to the Lord that they stayed there and taught these individuals for one year.

After these Antioch believers had been taught for one year about Jesus Christ, they were called Christians. In fact, this is the place where believers were first called Christians. They were Christian believers, not just believers. These Christians had been discipled about Jesus Christ.

A person who believes on the Lord, but does not turn to Him and the ways of His teachings, may very well be considered a believer. They have all the potential to do the *works*, and *greater works,* that Jesus did. They have the potential even though their everyday life, life-styles, and conversation may not necessarily reflect the fact that they are followers of Jesus.

On the other hand, a Christian believer is one who conscientiously endeavors to adhere to the ethics, values and morals of the character of Christ with an upright heart. Ingrained within these Christian principles comes a desire to demonstrate the power of the Holy Spirit through Jesus Christ while here on this earth. In other words, Christians are those individuals who endeavor to attain to do the *works,* or *greater works,* that Jesus said *believers* would do.

THE GREATEST WORK

We are qualified to enter into a deeper walk with Jesus and live a Christian life if we are a believer in Jesus Christ. We are the ones who make the decisions whether or not we will endeavor to attain to *the works* and *the greater works* Jesus said we could do. A Christian already will have made a decision to do these works. These *works* and *greater works* will be narrowed down in this text to refer to the works involving the power of the Holy Spirit. We need to take a closer look from this perspective to be able to ascertain what are the *works* and what are the *greater works* that Jesus expected believers would do.

I submit that the greatest work ever done by Jesus was when He was crucified on the cross for the sins of man. This was the Miracle of all miracles! After Jesus died He entered into the spirit realm of hell, a very real place where unsaved souls live out an eternal death. Satan thought that he had overcome the power of God when he saw

Christ in hell after He had been crucified on the cross. Mistake!

Jesus overcame the power that death had on His body. He was resurrected. He went to Hades and took the keys of hell and death from the devil. He rose again within the earth after three days. It was indeed the greatest work Jesus ever did. His death, resurrection, burial, and return to earth, clearly demonstrate that the power of death is subject to the power of God.

The fact that this is the greatest work ever done by Jesus should not be construed to mean that all believers must be crucified and resurrected in order to do greater works than Jesus. Only God's son, who was a perfect human vessel, would have to die on the cross to be a propitiation for the sins of mankind. Jesus was God's one and only choice. He was the only begotten Son of God and the only man to live on the earth who fit the description of a sinless man. This payment for the sin of mankind is a completed work that will never have to be duplicated by another human being.

The need now exists to look past the crucifixion and the resurrection of Jesus in order to ascertain the *greater works* since the redemptive work of Jesus never has to be repeated.

THE GREATER WORKS

One of the most notable works Jesus ever did was when He raised Lazarus from the dead (John 11:1-45). This man named Lazarus, a close friend of Jesus, became ill and died. Jesus had been summoned to come see Lazarus while he was sick, but He did not arrive until after Lazarus had been dead for four days. Lazarus had already been placed in his grave, which in this instance was a cave.

Jesus went to this grave-site once He arrived. He commanded others to roll away the stone from the opening of the cave. Jesus then invoked the power of the God by commanding, *Lazarus, come forth*. The Word of God tells us that *he that was dead came forth...* (John 11:43).

One of the works Jesus did is illuminated through this story. He raised the dead. Jesus said believers would do greater than this. Jesus did not say that believers *might* do greater works than He did. He prophetically declared that believers **will** do greater works than He did while He was upon this earth.

The fact that believers will do greater than Jesus should not be construed to mean that believers would have any greater power than Jesus. This Scripture should be construed more in terms of time instead of power. In other words, believers would be around on the earth much longer to demonstrate these works than Jesus since He was going to go be with the Father. Believers would have more occasion to demonstrate the works of God which, understandably, would allow them to do greater works than Jesus.

It is safe to deduce from Lazarus' example that Christian believers are potentially capable of raising the dead at least four days after someone has died. Let the gravity of this statement sink in for just a moment. A deceased person is usually in their grave within four days; at least in the western world. But what if they are not in their grave? Would we be willing to pray? So what if they were in their grave? Would we still be willing to pray and call them forth out of their grave like Jesus did?

Taking this example one step further, a body usually stinks from the decomposition process. Foul odors can still be emitted even if a corpse is embalmed. We know from Martha's comments that Lazarus' body stank. Regardless of any and all such hindering factors from our perspective, these factors are not an obstacle to God. They can be overridden when the necessary and unconventional faith is exercised on our part. Remember, Jesus would not tell believers to do *greater works* if we were not going to be challenged to do so — and if we were not capable of successfully accomplishing this.

WHY FOUR DAYS?

It is interesting to note, for a couple of reasons, why Jesus waited until Lazarus had been dead for four days before He came to raise him up. One of these reasons correlates to the Hebraic culture of that day and time. "Most rabbis held theories about the impossibility of resuscitation after three or four days of death."[1] Many people would have probably doubted the resurrection power of God had Jesus arrived to raise Lazarus any sooner. Lazarus' raising would have been viewed more as an act of the grace of God instead of the resurrection miracle that it was. The fact that Lazarus was raised when he was, was staggering to the people. Only the power of God could have caused such a miraculous occurrence to transpire.

Another possible reason Jesus might have delayed until the fourth day to raise Lazarus pertains to the people of our culture today. Believers today acknowledge that Jesus was raised from the dead after three days. Perhaps Jesus waited an extra day to raise Lazarus so Christians of today would not limit themselves to raising the dead to just three days. Stated another way, believers might possibly limit themselves to three days in believing God to raise an individual in that we would not want to exalt ourselves past Jesus. Regardless of His reason for waiting, Jesus' true fathering Spirit comes through in His four-day example of Lazarus. And just think, He wants believers to do *even greater* than this.

A LITERAL RESURRECTION

Jesus did His part by raising others from the dead and then, the more so, by being resurrected from the dead Himself. Now it is time for Christian believers to begin doing our part. We do not have to be raised from the dead physically to do the greater works Jesus did. Our minds and spirits, however, do need to be resurrected so we can attain to this dimension of greater works where raising the dead is concerned.

---

1. *Evangelical Commentary on the Bible*, Baker Book House: Grand Rapids, MI, 1989, p.863.

We have now been provided with a biblical basis of recourse from which to springboard into this dimension. Now we can begin to clear the path of a few distortions which have prevented us from seeing into this dimension more clearly.

CHAPTER THREE

~

APPOINTED ONCE
TO DIE

*"And as it is appointed for men to die once, but
after this the judgment,..."*

Hebrews 9:27

Sunday morning, September 9, 2001, two days before September
11 went down in infamy, I was joyfully worshiping the Lord in a Sunday
morning service, along with many others, to the tune of a lively,
Caribbean style song. The song was so vibrant that the men of the
church were invited by the leader to come down to the front so they
could have greater freedom to express themselves in dance. Several
men accepted that invitation. One particular gentleman turned to
another man, while joyfully praising God, and said, *This is so much*

fun! Shortly after making this statement, this man dropped to the floor, unconscious.

A calm chaos began to unfold as medical personnel in the congregation were summoned forward, and the pastor asked someone to call 911. The praise and worship service continued; however, it was somewhat strained, to say the least. Emergency medical technicians (EMT) arrived several minutes later and requested silence from the praise and worship in the auditorium. They immediately began administering CPR and using a defibrillator on the gentleman. They continued these procedures while leaving the church for the hospital.

The congregation was requested to come to the altar to intercede for this gentleman after the ambulance left to take him to the hospital. We did not yet know whether the man was dead or alive. Numerous attempts by the EMTs to save his life appeared to prove futile. The man did not respond to any of their procedures.

The thoughts running through my spirit at that time are clear and indelible. The fact that death occurred in the House of God on the Lord's Day was an insult. This is a place where the Body of Christ comes expecting to have life poured into them, not death. The atmosphere in the church was as if the devil had rendered God's people powerless, even though there was much prayer and declaring of the word of the Lord. It became progressively apparent that the Body of Christ would have to come to a place where we know how to respond with even more maturity in using our authority in the face of death. We would have to learn how to *work the miracle* rather than simply pray the prayer.

I specifically remember asking God one particular question while I was at the altar praying for this man. My question was, *If we are supposed to raise the dead, then how do we do it?* My spirit was on overload with other questions. *What do we do? How do we get to that place where we begin to see the dead raised to the glory of God? Where do we start?* God responded in the midst of all these questions by dropping a seed into my spirit that day.

The congregation was informed at the end of the service that the gentleman had been officially pronounced dead upon arrival at the hospital, and that funeral arrangements would be forthcoming. STOP RIGHT HERE! It is at this very pivotal point that we should let the realization dawn on us that there are other arrangements that can be made as well. Resurrection arrangements can also be interjected in the process.

These arrangements will have to happen if those who die a premature death are going to be raised! But, we will somehow have to manage to get inside these situations in order to intervene. Intervention in this manner will truly require what I will term at this point in time, some "unconventional" decisions and actions.

WHAT NOW?

How would you respond if you saw someone fall and exhibit no signs of life? Where would you go from there? What would you do? Would you automatically accept the death and expect funeral announcements to be forthcoming? Or, would you possibly be prepared to entertain the thought of another option when someone is pronounced dead? Would you be adequately prepared, whether as a loved one or a minister, to make other arrangements past the pronouncement of death in order to see that the deceased is raised? It is my hope that upon reading this book, answers to these questions will become much clearer and you will be much more likely to act.

ARE THEY DYING OR DEAD?

As various people found out what I was writing about, I quickly discovered that many of them had a different perception about the content of my book. What they perceived and what I was actually writing about were two different things. People conveyed stories to me about dying individuals they prayed over, and how God restored their life. These were no doubt truly miraculous stories, but their definition of being raised from the dead, and mine, were different. I could see that a distinction between the two terms needed to be made.

The word *dead* means no longer alive or having lost all life. *Dead* refers to someone, whose natural body is past the natural means of reviving. According to this definition, this is not inclusive of individuals whose lives are within the time frame for CPR. Neither does this definition include individuals whose life is being sustained through a life-support system or who still maintain some semblance of life. Individuals such as these fit the description of those considered to be *dying*, but not *dead*.

The need to make a distinction between those who are *dead* as opposed to those who are *dying* can best be summed with a real life example. A person who was knowledgeable about this writing sent word via my husband to inquire if I would be willing to come and pray for an individual who was on a life support system. Due to situations within our ministry, I did not speak with this minister concerning their inquiry until a day and a half later. My intentions were to minister life to this individual, but the need existed to first share my thoughts with the minister to ensure that we were on the same page in our definitions, especially if matters changed for the worse.

When I made efforts to initiate conversation, it was immediately conveyed to me that the plug on the life support machine had already been pulled. Like many, the extent of the existing belief system stopped at the point of believing God to raise a dying person when, in fact, it should be inclusive of ministry after a plug has been pulled.

Our natural tendency is to think of a dying person in terms of a dead person. Therefore, we think that we have already prayed for a dead person to be raised when in reality we prayed for a dying person. Praying for a dead person can escape our mentality and spiritual comprehension. In essence, prayer for dying individuals has been the picture of the corporate Church praying for the *dead* to be raised, up until this time. However, this fact will gradually begin to change.

Preparation to minister to deceased individuals is necessary if the Church is going to spiritually advance in this dimension. A prime example is a readiness to minister after life support is terminated. God is still God and a miracle is still a miracle whether God raises people from a dying bed, or after they have died and passed into the spirit realm.

Raising the dead may have sounded exciting up until this point but let's begin to temper our emotions even more with the sobering reality that we will have to cross some unconventional lines. The reaction to ministering to someone who is literally **dead** gives us an indication of just how much we need to further educate ourselves and prepare for this dimension. The fact may not dawn on believers that ministering to an individual does not have to stop upon their death. This option opens up another world of ministry.

Each death situation will be accompanied with its own unique set of challenges; both the fixed mental attitude of ourselves and that of unbelievers who may be directly involved with us. Christians will need to become better prepared to meet these challenges head on. Along this same line, the gravity of the following statement cannot be adequately conveyed with words. *Christians would be wise to expect that they might possibly encounter some very precarious situations when it comes to approaching deceased individuals, especially around unbelievers and unbelieving believers.*

Unbelief can be masked in many faces, forms, and fashions within an emotionally charged situation such as death. Christians should be aware and prepare as much as possible, in light of this fact, to know what may be required and expected of them when entering into these situations if the dead are indeed going to be raised.

RAISING THE BAR

The reality will continue to impress upon us, that we will be forced to cut across existing barriers of unbelief in order to approach deceased individuals to command the spirit of death off of a deceased. As we shall see, the peripheral circumstances cannot be allowed to become a hindrance to us when we determine in our spirit to enter into one of these situations. We will more fully recognize the impact of this statement once we begin entering into actual situations.

Are we perhaps ready to raise the bar of consideration for cutting-edge ministry with these thoughts in mind? If so, let this truth drop down in your spirit. We should become willing to approach deceased individuals like we would a dying individual. And remember, one is truly dead when they have finished dying.

REMOVING THE DOUBT

The purpose for making a distinction between dying and dead is not to split hairs. As previously stated, God is God whether a dying person is healed or a deceased person is raised. Miracles of dying persons being healed can be as remarkable as raisings from the dead. However, there is one distinction between the two that becomes important and is revealed in the midst of these two scenarios.

God should ideally receive all the glory from individuals when a healing or raising miracle takes place. Often that happens. Sometimes it does not. When a dying person is healed, there is a tendency for unbelievers or unbelieving believers to rationalize that the human body healed itself and God had nothing to do with the restoration. They can attribute the person's healing to the hands of a great physician or to the body's incredible ability to heal itself. The point being made is that there is room for doubt and disbelief that God had anything to do with a dying person being healed.

When a deceased individual is raised from the dead and returns to a normal life among men, the irrefutable outcome is that only God Almighty could have intervened. God cannot help but receive the credit from those who would choose to doubt otherwise when a true raising takes place. Only an unbelieving, lost soul could deny the power of God when presented with the miraculous power of God in this way.

The need to remove the doubt of whether a person was truly dead or not does not stop after the actual resurrection either. Miraculous stories such as these spread like wildfire. People listening to these stories will want to be credibly assured that an individual was indeed dead. If it is not already apparent, one of the first responses from the hearers of such a story will be to ask if the person was really dead. People usually need reliable facts before readily accepting such a story as truth.

The key factor that establishes credibility for the unbeliever in these stories is the fact that the individual who was raised was verifiably dead. There may be times when a death is not credibly verifiable by others and this is okay. Just because there is not a piece of paper to verify the death does not make it any less of a miracle. A natural life was still restored regardless of who chose to believe the story.

We could lose focus if not careful and slip into the mode of trying to convince unbelievers about the power of God. Our focus should remain on exercising faith in order to see the resurrection power of God restore a life. The power of God will speak for itself in these situations to those who chose to believe in such a miracle.

AN APPOINTMENT WITH DEATH

There is no doubt that the soul and spirit have entered another spirit realm of heaven or hell when an individual is truly dead. It is my wish for you to choose to accept Jesus Christ as your personal Savior, and for you to have evidence of a godly life when you pass through the portal of death. Heaven is a place where our life is lived out eternally. Hell is a place where a living death is lived out eternally.

John 3:16 states, *"For God so loved the world that He gave His only begotten Son, that whoever believes in Him should not perish but have everlasting life."* We know those who truly believe in Christ Jesus as their Lord and Savior will be granted eternal life into heaven. Others will live out an eternal death. Acts 2:21 and Romans 10:13 states that whoever shall call upon the name of the Lord shall be saved.

Only God knows the heart of those who truly believe in Jesus Christ. Calling upon the name of the Lord may come across as a minor decision or trivial detail, but it will, in fact, determine your eternal destination of heaven or hell. The people who call upon the Lord Jesus Christ will be protected from an eternal death when they die and pass through the portal of death into heaven and eternal life. Those who do not, sadly stated, go to hell.

Regardless of where the soul of a deceased goes after one dies, relatives and friends of the deceased in the meantime are left behind on earth struggling to cope with the loss. They usually cope by searching for any explainable or plausible responses to justify the death.

APPOINTED TO DIE

One traditional response to death that merits being addressed in this text is found in Hebrews 9:27, *"...it is appointed for men to die once,..."* Let's take a moment to closely examine this Scripture.

Re-read this verse and think about what it is conveying. When you think about it, this verse merely addresses the fact that everyone will have to die an earthly death at least once. This fact makes sense in that sinful flesh must be shed before a person's spirit can ever enter into the perfect realm of heaven. The intended meaning of this Scripture, however, in no way focuses on the timeliness of a death. We are appointed to die one time, but *when* we die is a totally different issue. The issue of *when* we die is not addressed at all.

The intended meaning to be gleaned from this Scripture is that we all have an appointment with death at least once. Well-intentioned ministers and others often misinterpret and misapply this verse, especially at funerals. They interpret the Scripture to mean that a man will die only one time and since this particular person has died they use this Scripture to imply that it was an *appointed time* to die. In essence, this verse is often misconstrued and used to mean that all deaths are timely. Raising the dead would not even be an option for consideration if all deaths are timely. If raising the dead is an option, a person can, in fact, die more than one time.

Raising the dead would not even be an option for consideration if all deaths are timely.

Would Jesus have raised Lazarus, a ruler's daughter (Matthew 9:18-25), or a widow's son (Luke 7:11-17) if all deaths are considered *timely*? Of course He would not. He does not work against Himself. Jesus was demonstrating how believers could operate in this dimension in the event someone died a premature death. Accordingly, the usage of Hebrews 9:27 over a deceased should be considered an appropriate response in the event of a plausible death and not as a crutch to justify a premature one.

The need exists among believers to arrive at the conclusion that not every death happens at an appointed time. The realization should be dawning on us that we have a God-given right to question whether or not we think a person's death was premature. The fact that we can question the timeliness of a death is the first step in beginning to move toward raising the dead.

DEATH AND DESTINY
Another initial issue that might quickly surface when someone

dies is the question of that person's destiny being fulfilled. The word *destiny* is one of those terms having mass application on a broad scale. It applies to all individuals to some degree or another. Thus, there are a number of ways that the word *destiny* can be defined, depending on your fundamental perspective on life.

For purposes of this writing, the word *destiny* will be used to mean the following: *the fulfilling of godly purpose in a person's life before the True God of Heaven, given one's human will, abilities and confines.* Given this definition, it becomes clear that, as long as the One, True God, is alive, we all have destiny to be fulfilling. Hopefully, it will be inclusive of godly purposes.

The mere definition of *destiny* infers that we should have somewhere to go and something to be doing because we have purpose in the earth for the Kingdom of God. We only have to look at the small and large of our decisions on a daily basis to see where we are headed in order to accomplish what we know we have to do. These everyday decisions chart the road we travel and the overall path we take in living before the Lord, our God.

Ideally, we walk in our earthly destiny and continue fulfilling it, even though we do not know what all that entails as we navigate through this life. For example, this book, in all probability, would not have been written had it not been prophesied to me. The prophetic word of the Lord handed me further meaning and ongoing purpose I never expected! However, I was in the right place at the right time fulfilling destiny that particular day because I chose to be at the House of the Lord on the Sabbath. While at church fulfilling destiny, I was handed further destiny of purpose through the prophetic word that would forever chart and change the direction of my personal life — big time!

As you can see, destiny is not just about where we are and a specific destination. It is about where we are headed as we navigate through this life on a daily basis and what may come our way. Stated another way, it is about the journey we walk out during our sojourn on this earth. In light of the given definition, are we doing what we know to do that will put us on the everyday beat and path to fulfilling godly purpose in our life, given our human will, abilities and limitations?

CONFORMED TO HIS IMAGE

In Romans 8:29, the Apostle Paul alludes to a certain aspect of our destiny before we were ever born when he stated:

> *"For whom He foreknew, He also predestined to be conformed to the image of His Son."*
>
> Romans 8:29

Needless to say, God foreknew all of us before we were born. It is in the very fiber of our being to be conformed to the image of Jesus. We were predestined to be like the very image of Jesus. This does not mean that because Jesus was a carpenter that we should all be carpenters.

In the process of fulfilling destiny, in whatever we choose to be, we should endeavor to be like Jesus. In other words, we should strive to allow the character of Jesus Christ to be formed within us while living on the earth. While we may or may not know a specific role or function in which to carry out our destiny, we know how we should go about fulfilling it. We should fulfill it in such a way that we are conformed to the character of Christ.

Sadly enough, not all choose such a path. Ideally, each of us should live out our lives so that it reflects who Jesus Christ is in us. If we know we have been predestined to be conformed to the image of Jesus Christ, then our everyday life and life-style should reflect that destiny in whatever arena in which we find ourselves. What we choose to do in life, and how we daily live out that fact reveals an unfolding degree of destiny in our journey.

GOD'S WILL BE DONE

God's will is for godly destiny to be fulfilled in each and every life to the fullest extent humanly possible while upon this earth. Only God knows when an individual's destiny is as complete as it is going to be before they leave this earth. Ideally, we should exit this earth like Jesus; when it can be said that our godly purpose for being on this earth is finished.

All too often individuals may exit this earth and their work is not finished. For example, Ecclesiastes 7:17 says, *"Do not be overly wicked, Nor be foolish: Why should you die before your time?"* People can be overly wicked or act foolish and it may cause them to die before their work is finished. The Apostle Paul provides us with another example in 1 Corinthians 5:1-5 of how someone may end up dying before their time.

Paul received a report that sexual immorality was being tolerated in the Corinthian church. A man had taken his father's wife. Paul judged this deed in verse 5 because the church there did not. He instructed the church leaders to *"...deliver such a one to Satan for the destruction of the flesh, that his spirit may be saved in the day of the Lord Jesus."* As we can see, someone may die early so that their soul may be saved.

Another reason someone may die before their time is found in Isaiah 57:1-2. *The Living Bible* translation says, *"The good men perish, the godly die before their time, and no one seems to care or wonder why. No one seems to realize that God is taking them away from evil days ahead. For the godly who die shall rest in peace."* In other words, God will take men away in order to avoid evil days that may lie ahead of them.

There are some things we can do so we will not die before our time. On the other hand, nothing can be done if God chooses to remove someone from this earth in order to avoid future evil, or, He allows for the destruction of their flesh so that their spirit will be saved. In essence, these particular scriptures reveal that there are biblical reasons for why someone may die early.

Also illuminated within the aforementioned scriptures is the fact that there are valid reasons for why a deceased may not be raised upon receiving resurrection ministry. It is for scriptures like these that we should, all the more, learn to tune in to hear God's voice and get the mind of Christ within the midst of each and every seemingly premature death situation we encounter. We can minister for hours over a deceased who, unknown to us, God chose to remove from this earth. No matter how much and how long we exercise our faith, they still will not be raised against God's will.

Given this fact, we should avoid the temptation of assuming that a deceased will be raised just because they are receiving ministry from faith-filled ministers. And, we should avoid making the same assumption that just because we perceive that a deceased's work on earth was not finished that they will be raised. The best assumption that we can make in these situations is that God's will will be done, and not ours. This outcome is regardless of our heartfelt desires.

Whether we finish our earthly work like Jesus did, or, we are not able to finish, only God knows for certain. In the meantime, we should all aspire to further fulfill Godly destiny in our everyday lives. This is inclusive of living a Godly lifestyle, and not one that would preclude us from staying our course and finishing the race set before us.

A BIBLICAL APPROACH

An unfolding path of questions and answers regarding this dimension lies ahead for the Body of Christ. This path will take us past some of the traditional mindsets handed to us about death and destiny. As we will see, there are many more non-traditional responses and behaviors that believers will need to take in order to see that a deceased is raised. These responses and behaviors will be challenged by those believers who, whether knowingly or unknowingly, desire to maintain the status quo responses when someone dies.

Cutting edge believers will be pressed to go beyond the perceptions of what many deem "decent and in order" Christianity when someone dies a premature death. This will become especially evident when living loved ones left behind desire resurrection ministry for their deceased loved one.

Acknowledging this fact with your "third ear" is a big step. This fact alone should provoke us to think about making preparation now as to how we would realistically enter into these situations. In other words, what needs to happen in order for ministers to get inside these situations, and, how we would go about ministering to the deceased?

The first thing we should do to prepare to enter into one of these situations in a biblical manner is really simple. First and foremost, we should go to the Bible and observe the responses and actions of Jesus when He encountered a premature death situation. We should take note of what Jesus did and let His actions be a example to us.

CHAPTER FOUR

~

WHAT DID JESUS DO?

"Why should you die before your time?"
Ecclesiastes 7:17b

In the terms of the writer of Ecclesiastes, how do we know when someone dies "before (their) time?" How can we know when someone dies before their time if we do not even know when they are going to die to begin with? The bottom line here is that only God knows when we are going to die, therefore, only He knows for sure when someone dies before their time. Given this fact, any rigid, conclusive criteria we would attempt to establish to ascertain a death as premature would be in vain.

Having said this, if Jesus told us to raise the dead, it is up to us to learn how to wisely move into death situations. Granted, moving into death situations will require us to make some decisions that may not be easy. For this reason, wisdom dictates that we first resort to the Scriptures since they are our most reliable source for revelation and wisdom. Specifically, we should take Jesus as our example and observe how He became involved in death situations.

What compelled Jesus to make the decision to enter into these situations? How was He drawn into these situations? We will see that issues like the timing of a person's death, and whether or not a person's destiny was fulfilled, were not addressed. The answers to these questions are more in keeping with the issues of faith, compassion and love.

BIBLICAL PREMATURE DEATHS

There are a few stories in the Bible of certain individuals who were raised from the dead to the glory of God. The New Testament stories involving Jesus best illustrate how living loved ones and ministers might respond when death situations cross our path. The morsels of truth gleaned from these stories should become foundational stepping stones for gaining spiritual insight and wisdom on moving into these situations.

We have record in the New Testament of Jesus raising three people from the dead. There is also one story where Jesus could have easily prayed for a deceased but chose not to do so. We will note in the first three stories how the living loved ones and Jesus reacted and responded to situations of death when it crossed their path. Particular note should be taken of how Jesus responded when He approached a deceased person. We also need to recognize the important fact that, even when Jesus was not approached, He still ministered life.

In order to more fully complement the above-mentioned stories where Jesus willingly entered into these situations, we will see in one story why Jesus did not take the liberty to minister to a deceased when He could have easily stepped forward to do so. We, as believers, can get a better handle on what may also compel us to enter into these situations after carefully observing the reactions and responses of the individuals in the following four stories.

JAIRUS' YOUNG DAUGHTER

The first story is found in Matthew 9:18-26 and Luke 8:40-56. It involves a living loved one named Jairus. Jairus was a young ruler of a synagogue whose twelve-year-old daughter became very sick. He set out to find Jesus to come minister life to her very sick body. The account in Luke states that when Jairus found Jesus, he begged Him to come to his house. Jairus received word at about the same time that his daughter died.

Notice the immediate response of Jesus upon hearing this fact. Jesus responded to the ruler in Luke 8:50 by saying, *"Do not be afraid; only believe, and she will be made well."* Jesus further encouraged him to continue believing even after being informed that his daughter was dead. We see here that Jesus did not stop to question the circumstances surrounding her death, nor its timing. Instead, He chose to see faith. He recognized that Jairus sought Him out because he believed Jesus could make his young daughter well.

Jairus wanted his little girl made whole and he took actions of faith to find Jesus for this purpose. Jesus honored this man's continuing faith. He did not pose any questions to Jairus about the little girl. The first words He spoke is that the young girl would *"be made well"*. He backed up His words with action and made plans to go to Jairus' house to minister to his daughter. The fact that she died was not a signal to make funeral plans. It should not always be a signal to us either.

As the living loved one, Jairus had the authority to permit or prevent Jesus from coming to his house. Obviously, Jairus allowed Him to come to his house for the purpose of commanding life to return to her body. In short, life was restored to the young girl's body after Jesus commanded her to "arise".

As you can see, Jesus was primarily compelled to enter into this situation based initially on seeing the faith of Jairus. He did not try to ascertain any facts about the timeliness of the girl's death. No justifiable statements such as her death was "to the glory of God" or it was "God's time" were ever mentioned. No, He responded with faith to meet Jairus' faith.

There is one major and important word of wisdom to glean from this story. We should learn to react and respond to the faith that we see in living loved ones who approach us as a basis for moving into these situations. On the other hand, the only faith being generated may come from a believer who is not the living loved one. This is evidenced in our second story.

THE WIDOW AT NAIN

The second story is found in Luke 7:11-15. We find Jesus, and a large crowd with Him, about to enter into the gates of a city called Nain. Jesus encountered a funeral procession coming out of the gate as He was about to enter. It was the funeral procession of a young man.

The Scripture reveals that this young man was the only son of his widowed mother. Verse 13 tells us, *"When the Lord saw her, He had compassion on her and said to her, 'Do not weep.'"* Take note here that Jesus was drawn by the Spirit of God to enter into this situation based on compassion. Jesus reacted and responded because of the compassion He had for this widowed woman/mother when He saw her heart-broken condition.

We are provided very little information about this man, except that he was his mother's only son. We do not see Jesus trying to ascertain information about this man and whether he should be raised or not. The Scripture reveals to us that this man was raised purely out of the compassion and faith Jesus had on behalf of the young man's mother.

As we reflect on this particular story, we are made aware that we may be more motivated to react and respond out of a heart of compassion and faith for surviving family members instead of the deceased. Interestingly enough, issues pertaining to the death of the deceased may not have anything to do with why they may be raised. The timing of this man's death, or even his destiny being further fulfilled, were not the obvious considerations. The compassion Jesus had for the man's mother was obviously the compelling consideration for reacting and responding the way He did in this situation.

Both of the prior stories revealed how Jesus was first motivated to step forward by recognizing and responding to the faith of living loved ones, and when He was moved with compassion. These were people who He did not know and who did not know Him. In other words, He reacted and responded in this manner to individuals with whom He had no prior relationship. In other words, Jesus was not personally and emotionally attached to the people in the situations, in the strict sense of the words.

Let's observe how Jesus reacted and responded, and what compelled Him to react and respond when it was someone He knew.

LAZARUS COMES FORTH

This story is perhaps the most well known story in biblical circles where a deceased person was raised, other than the resurrection of Jesus. We briefly discussed this story in *Chapter Two*, but let's take a look at some more facts in order to understand it from another perspective. It is a story involving two sisters, named Mary and Martha, and their brother, Lazarus. Lazarus became very sick and eventually died.

We see that the primary and motivating force that compelled Jesus to react and respond to Lazarus' death is revealed almost from the outset of the story in John 11. Verse 3 of John 11 states, *"Therefore the sisters sent to Him, saying,"Lord, behold, he whom You love is sick."* Verse 5 goes on to state, *"Now Jesus loved Martha and her sister and Lazarus."* In essence, Jesus automatically responded and reacted to attend to this situation out of a heart of love for this family. By the time He finally arrived at their house, Lazarus had already died.

The first thing Jesus did was to individually and respectively talk to Martha and Mary. Unlike the story of Jairus, where Jesus addressed the man's fear, Jesus began addressing Martha and Mary's faith. (This issue will be further addressed in *Chapter Seventeen*). Even though Jesus had been in their house many times, and they were very close to Him, they still could not discern the enormous significance of His being, and what He could do.

After meeting with Mary and Martha individually, Jesus was taken straight to the place where Lazarus had been buried. Those famous words still resonate loud and clear among Christian circles today, when Jesus called Lazarus to *"Come forth!"* out of the darkness of his grave. We know that Lazarus came forth but, back to our main question, what first motivated Jesus to get involved in this situation?

The same thing that first compelled Jesus to get involved in this situation is the same thing that would compel you and me if someone close to us died. It is our relational love for them, not to mention the looming elements of faith and compassion. Jesus did not bring up issues of whether He thought Lazarus should or should not be raised. The only reasoning Jesus needed to raise Lazarus was faith.

Did Jesus step forward to call Lazarus forth because Mary and Martha were so upset? Did he pray because Lazarus was his friend? Do you think Jesus was compelled to step forward out of a heart of relational love for this family? Yes, to all three questions. Jesus was primarily compelled to attend to this situation out of His closeness and love for this family.

FAITH, COMPASSION, AND LOVE

Clearly, faith was initiated and exercised in all three stories. Jairus initiated his faith as he sought out Jesus. Jesus further responded with His faith to see that the girl was resurrected. Jesus was also clearly responsible for initiating and exercising His faith in order to see that the widow's son and Lazarus were also resurrected. His faith was in response to the compassion and love for how the relating individuals were affected.

He helped a father who could only exercise so much faith by asking Jesus to come to his house. He further helped a widow who could not even help herself. He took it upon himself to cover his friends' lack of faith by exercising His faith on their behalf. In short, His actions were predicated upon compassion and love, not what He could ascertain about the deceased.

In summary, the example of Jesus provides us with some key insights and morsels of wisdom for stepping out in this dimension. When we step out to exercise our faith to raise the dead, it may be a reciprocated act that is predicated upon seeing the faith of others who approach us. Compassion for the hopeless and helpless living loved ones is another scriptural reason for initiated action. The last insight is that of our love for the individuals who seemingly are willing but cannot help themselves.

COMMANDING LIFE TO COME

Let's take note of one common thread that runs throughout these three stories. Notice how Jesus addressed all three deceased individuals. He said to Jairus' daughter, *"Little girl, arise."* The widow's son was addressed by Jesus saying, *"Young man, I say to you arise."* Jesus personally addressed Lazarus since He knew him. He said, *"Lazarus, come forth!"* Notice that all of these expressions were given in the form of a command, and not necessarily a prayer.

Jesus had already prayed before he called Lazarus to come forth, as seen in John 11:41. He said, *"Father, I thank You that You have heard Me."* He already had to be prayed up when He came upon Jairus' daughter, and especially in the situation of the widow's son. He was ready for these situations as they crossed His path. He knew that the Father had already heard Him.

In essence, Jesus wisely spent His time in these situations by directly addressing the deceased individuals, and not other spirits associated with death and hell. He commanded life to come when He told *the deceased* what to do. Death had no choice but to leave when this happened. All three deceased individuals immediately returned to the earthly realm upon His commands.

Likewise, we should take note from the example of Jesus. Jesus went into these situations having already prayed. He commanded life to come forth when He was ministering. He did not ask in prayer. Likewise, we should focus on what we want the Lord to do for the deceased in these situations. The spirits of death and hell will have to line up according to the authority of our commands.

WHEN JESUS DIDN'T RESPOND

We have discussed what compelled Jesus to respond and react when presented with certain situations of death where individuals were raised. But, what caused Him not to respond when a death situation crossed His path? In order to answer that question we have to keep in mind what caused Him to respond: faith, compassion and love. When we keep these factors central in our thinking, it will clue us in on how we might respond or react to situations of death.

Jesus provided us with some insight into questions of this issue in Matthew 8:19-22.

19"""Then a certain scribe came and said to Him,

"Teacher, I will follow You wherever You go."

²⁰And Jesus said to him, "Foxes have holes and birds of the air have nests, but the Son of Man has no where to lay His head."

²¹Then another of His disciples said to Him, "Lord, let me first go and bury my father."

²²But Jesus said to him, "Follow Me, and let the dead bury their own dead."'

Jesus creatively used the word "dead" two times here. He used it in the figurative sense and a literal sense in order to get His point across. Figuratively speaking, Jesus used the first appearance of the word "dead" to refer to individuals who could not spiritually comprehend the resurrection power of God operating through Jesus. The inability to respond with any kind of faith in this regard was born out by their actions. These were the people who automatically buried their literally deceased loved ones without any regard for the possibility of being raised through Jesus.

When Jesus used the word *"dead"* the second time, He was, in essence, instructing us in this Scripture to let people like this go ahead and bury their deceased loved ones. For example, Jesus could have said to this particular man, "Would you like for me to go with you and minister to your father?" Or, "Let's go and minister to your father that he may be raised to life again". As you well know, Jesus did not do this. Why? The answer to this question possibly lies in the man's one revealing statement to Jesus.

The man said, "*...let me first go and bury my father.*" Catch this point. The man's faith was in burying his father. Jesus did not see any faith to respond to in this situation. No faith was present for raising his father from the dead, and Jesus did not override this fact. The elements of faith, compassion and love were not present to the degree that Jesus was compelled to respond or react any other way. He merely said, *"let the dead bury their own dead."*

We would be wise to take note of Jesus' actions in this situation and apply them from another perspective as well. Just because we may know how to go about raising the dead does not mean that we should just go and arbitrarily place ourselves in morgues, funeral homes and places of death. This would not be wise, and it does not appear to be in line with the example of Jesus' approach into these situations.

In light of the previous stories from the Bible, it is obvious that Jesus did not go looking for death. If anything, we can see that situations of this sort crossed the path of His everyday life. Simply stated, death situations found Jesus. He did not go seeking them. Likewise, we would be wise to allow this pattern to take shape in our lives and learn to react and respond like Jesus did.

We know that Jesus had all the faith He needed to raise the dead. In this case though, there evidently was not the necessary degree of faith, compassion, or relational love present to compel Jesus to react and respond with actions for raising this man's father. Our thinking should be predicated upon these same foundational truths.

Like Jesus, we should indeed let the dead bury their own dead, but let those who are alive in Christ raise the dead when the elements of faith, compassion and/or love compel us to enter into these situations.

OUR SPIRITUAL SENSES EXERCISED

There is one last morsel of wisdom and insight here that should remain central in our spirits when considering how we might respond to these situations. Jesus provides us with this morsel in John 5:19. He says, *"Most assuredly, I say to you, the Son can do nothing of Himself,* **but what He sees the Father do**; *for whatever He does, the Son also does in like manner."'* (emphasis added).

Jesus was so connected to His Father that He did not do anything except what He saw Him do. Usually, we do not naturally see with our natural eyes what our heavenly Father does. We see with the eyes of our spirit and spiritual understanding. In order to better see what the Father does, our prayer before entering in to one of these situations should be like the one Jesus prayed in the Garden of Gethsemane before He went to the cross (Matthew 26:38). He prayed, "*...nevertheless, not as I will, but as you will.*"

May these two Scriptures be a leading lamp unto our feet and a guiding light unto our path.

WHAT IS NOT SAID

The purpose for this chapter is to reveal how Jesus, our example, reacted and responded when situations of death crossed His path. We have taken note of what was said in these situations, but what about what was not said? We should stop and give credence to what was not said.

We have no knowledge that Jesus stopped to ascertain details about any of the deceased individuals before He raised them. Our tendency is to think that biblical writers like Matthew, Luke and John would have been inspired by the Holy Spirit to provide us with some wisdom and insight in this direction. It is evidenced within the Scriptures that they did not.

What these writers were inspired to provide for us when entering into one of these situations is simple. Our responses are ones that should be predicated upon responding to the faith of others, having compassion for the living loved ones, and the love of God operating through us. Principles like these are what should primarily compel us to take action to raise the dead.

CHAPTER FIVE

~

FAITH, LOVE AND COMPASSION AT WORK

"To everything there is a season, a time for every purpose under heaven: a time to be born, and a time to die;..."

Ecclesiastes 3:1-2a

As the writer of Ecclesiastes states, there is *"a time to be born, and a time to die;..."* Sooner or later, we all have to die. As the old saying goes, everybody wants to go to heaven but nobody wants to die to get there. Generally speaking, we will have to die to get to heaven unless, of course, we are the end-time generation who is translated. Given the fact that we have to die, not every death can be considered premature since we are all appointed to die at least once. Given the fact that we are appointed to die, not every death can be considered premature. A death may very well be a plausible one.

PREMATURE DEATH AND PLAUSIBLE DEATH

A death can either be deemed plausible or premature. A small degree of insight was provided with regard to a premature death in the previous chapter but not on a plausible death. For purposes of this writing, let's begin by identifying just what we mean when we use the phrases *premature death* and *plausible death*.

The words, *premature death*, is a very nebulous phrase that only God can adequately define since He is the only one who knows when we are going to die. This means that we cannot attach a concrete definition to its meaning. For the sake of clarity within this writing, however, a working definition needs to be established. Generally speaking, let's just say that the phrase *premature death* infers that we think an individual should not have died as early as they did.

On the other hand, a *plausible death* is when we can begin to sense that an individual has ascended to the heavenly realm for the purpose of staying there. Overall, it may be safe to say that the person's plans and purposes for life may now better be served in the spirit realm. Further, we find ourselves ready and willing to release the person to the spirit realm.

Determining whether a death is *premature* or *plausible* can be a very complex issue. One way to somewhat simplify the nature of this issue from the outset is to predispose ourselves to some of the traditional and erroneous mind-sets that possibly could have been passed on to us. We could easily run the risk of confusing a *premature death* for a supposedly *plausible* one, and vice versa, if not adequately informed. As a word of admonition, we should not be too quick to ignore any sensing in our spirit with regard to the timing of an individual's death by jumping to any unfounded conclusions.

In Ephesians 1:17-18, the Apostle Paul asked that a spirit of revelation and wisdom in the knowledge of Him be given to the people at Ephesus and that the eyes of their understanding would be enlightened. We would be wise to ask God for the same in order to come to the best decision regarding a *premature* or *plausible* death. Naturally speaking, we can seriously begin to give some forethought to these issues now.

In other words, what thoughts might begin to surface if we actually had to prepare to enter into one of these situations? Are there any pre-existing mind-sets embedded in the recesses of our minds that could subconsciously become a stumbling block to our reactions and ways of responding? Would we know whether or not these mind-sets might subconsciously prevent us from responding out of faith, compassion and love?

With these questions in mind, let's take a look at a few issues that may have the potential to adversely affect our decisions and override our willingness and readiness to enter into these situations. We do not want to make hasty decisions that would keep our faith from coming forth.

THE DECEASED IS AN UNBELIEVER

It is important to remember that the ongoing concern for souls to be saved from hell should always remain central in the work of the Lord. This fact, especially in death situations, holds true where the eternal destiny of a soul may be hanging in the balances between heaven and hell. For this reason, one major issue we may need to initially resolve is our willingness to pray for deceased unbelievers to be raised.

A passage of Scripture in Luke 16:19-28 provides us with an interesting starting point on the issue of praying for unbelievers. This is a story about a rich man who died and his soul was sent to torment.[1] This man had not walked in the ways of the Lord. He was able to see

---

1. Since this story occurs before Jesus Christ's death and resurrection, the dead are being held in either Hades or a place referenced as Abraham's bosom, rather than in eternal hell and heaven, respectively.

another man, Lazarus, who had died around the same time standing "*afar off*" with Abraham. He cried out to Abraham, who was standing on the other side of a great gulf fixed between them. He asked Abraham to have mercy on him by sending over some water through a man named Lazarus.

The rich man wanted to dip the tip of his finger in water so he could cool his tongue because he was "*tormented in this flame*". Abraham responded by saying, "'*Son, remember that in your earthly lifetime you received your good things, and likewise Lazarus evil things; but now he is comforted and you are tormented. And besides all this, between us and you there is a great gulf fixed, so that those who want to pass from here to you cannot, nor can those from there pass to us.*'"

Realizing the gulf was "*fixed*," the rich man then begged Abraham to send Lazarus back to the earthly realm to tell his five brothers of his father's house about Jesus. He wanted his family to have no part in Hades and the torments in which they would ultimately find themselves if they died without knowing God.

This rich man knew he could not talk to his loved ones who were still alive on the earth. Apparently, he believed that since he was unable, Abraham could send Lazarus back to earth to warn his family.

Strict adherence to the principles within this story pertaining to the rich man, without the grace and sovereignty of God factored into the picture, would be to dismiss the tendency to pray for the spirit of an unbeliever to be returned to their body. The Bible explicitly states in this passage of Scripture that the gulf is "*fixed*" once an individual is retained in hell. *Once an individual is retained* is the key phrase.

We should not assume that just because an unsaved, or even a saved person dies, that their spirit is permanently retained in the spirit realm. If this were so, then raising the dead would not even be an option for consideration. God, and only God, in His infinite

knowledge, knows when the soul of an individual will be retained —
be it in heaven or hell. It is our obligation as maturing Christians to
have our spiritual senses exercised to hear God's will for the
individual's life.

Along this same line of thinking, we should, first and foremost,
remember that Jesus came to seek and save that which was lost. For
purposes of this discussion, if we thought that an individual who died
a premature death was going to live out life in eternal hell, all the
more reason to consider standing and believing for God to raise that
individual; so they could at least be given another opportunity to be
led to the Lord. 2 Peter 3:9 states that the Lord is *"not willing that any
should perish but that all should come to repentance."* If God is not willing
that one should perish, then neither should we, if we sense by the
Spirit of the Lord that we should minister.

In the meantime, we should totally avoid making a blanket
statement in saying that we should not pray for unbelievers to be
raised from the dead. Remember that all things are possible with
God, and God determines what is humanly expedient within His
infinite possibilities and purposes. If God wants life to return to a
non-believer, then so be it, according to our faith and the role we
play.

Has an unbeliever ever been raised from the dead by another
believer? Yes, according to Lay-Evangelist Dr. Bob Rice of Santa Fe,
New Mexico, in his book, *Holy Eucharist*.

AN UBELIEVER RAISED

One day Dr. Rice was called to a hospital to be with a family
from his church. This family had a nephew, who lived with them.
However, he was not a believer and did not attend any church. Upon
arriving at the hospital, the family informed Dr. Rice that the nephew
was already dead. He had been killed as a result of an automobile
accident. The California Highway Patrol said the man was dead. The

ambulance driver said he was dead and the hospital checked him and pronounced him dead on arrival.

The Lord spoke a rhema word to Dr. Rice and told him that if he went to the dead body and rebuked the death and commanded life to return to him, He would raise him up. Dr. Rice inquired as to the whereabouts of the body and asked the hospital personnel if he could have a few minutes alone with the deceased. The hospital personnel thought he was a grieving friend and granted him this request.

Dr. Rice, having never prayed for someone who was dead before, did what God told him to do. He laid his hands on the dead body, rebuked the death and commanded life to return to him. The next thing he knew was that this man came back to life. The hospital people came running in, and one of them said, "Get that tag off his toe" as they rushed him off to the emergency room.[2]

In essence, Dr. Rice was tuned into God to the degree that he heard the Spirit tell him to pray for the unbelieving man in a certain manner. God gave him a "rhema" word, and he was obedient to that directive from God. One more soul was snatched from the grips of hell because Dr. Rice was obedient to pray for an unbeliever. Likewise, we should remain receptive in our spirit to the sovereignty of God.

Additionally, if God ever uses you to raise up a non-believer, further responsibility exists to lead that person to the Lord Jesus Christ, according to John 3:16, for the purpose of securing their eternal salvation and destination in heaven. As a side note, if they got a taste of hell while in the spirit realm, leading them to Jesus might come much easier had they not died. If for no other reason than this, we should remain open to the sensing and promptings of the Holy Spirit to pray for a deceased, who was an unbeliever.

---

2. For those not familiar with standard hospital procedures in the U.S., the toe of a deceased individual is tagged for identification purposes before the corpse is sent to the morgue.

THE AGE FACTOR

Another common misconception relating to premature death pertains to the age factor. We should not be too quick to dismiss praying for a deceased just because of what we see in the natural, especially when the faith of the living loved ones is for the deceased to be raised. This is particularly true when it comes to the age of a deceased. What we see in that natural in the way of age can deceive us, unless we become otherwise informed on this issue. This is especially true if our thinking lines up with traditional teachings.

A traditional teaching concerning the expected life span of man has existed in the Church for years. It, in essence, teaches that we are entitled to live a life span of seventy to eighty years. It is important that this teaching be dispelled in order to make a more informed decision on raising the dead when it comes to age and a plausible death. Gloria Copeland has clearly shown the error of this traditional teaching.[3]

As best as can be ascertained, this teaching is premised upon Psalm 90:10. This verse states, *"The days of our lives are seventy years; And if by reason of strength they are eighty years."* This particular Scripture appears to back up this seventy-to-eighty-year mentality at face value, but you have to go back and look at this verse within the context of which it was written.

Psalm 90:9 lets us in on a little insight to the proper truth of this teaching. It states that, *"For all of our days have passed away in Your wrath; . . ."* We know that all of our days have not passed away in wrath — even though we may at times wonder. If this Scripture does not pertain to us today, then to whom is this Scripture alluding?

This Scripture is alluding to the complaining and rebellious children of God who would not do what He told them to do. They

---

3. Copeland, Gloria, *Believer's Voice of Victory, Live Life, Live Long Webcast, May 7, 2005.*

refused to enter into their promised land, Canaan, due to an overwhelmingly, bad report about the land (Numbers 14:26-35). As a result of their complaining and rebellious ways, God made a declaration that pertained to everyone twenty years and older.

He stated that, *"According to the number of the days in which you spied out the land, forty days, for each day you shall bear your guilt one year, namely forty years, and you shall know My rejection"* (Numbers 14:34). God was basically telling them that they would go into the wilderness for forty years and, in essence, would die off.

This was a whole generation that was sentenced to die. Verse 10 of Psalm 90 is basically conveying to us that most of these people who had been wandering around in the wilderness since they were twenty years or older, were now dying at age seventy. Additionally, they were living to be eighty years old if they were strong men. They were cursed to die and never see their promised land because they had tested God *"ten times"* (Numbers 14:22-23).

It is easy to see how this particular passage of Scripture in Psalms could be misconstrued and mistaken as a set span of life for mankind. However, this given life-span is simply not true. If there is anything specifically addressed in Scripture concerning the expected life-span of mankind, it is seen in Genesis 6:3. *"And the Lord said, "My Spirit shall not strive with man forever, for he is indeed flesh; yet his days shall be one hundred and twenty years."*

We see in this passage of Scripture, that God shortened the life-span of man from over nine hundred years (Genesis 5) to live to be one hundred twenty years. If anything, we can biblically aspire to live to be one hundred twenty years if we so choose. Many may not want to live that long, but at least the option has been afforded us by God for those who aspire to live as long a life as possible.

This mentality that we should only expect to live between seventy and eighty years of age needs to be removed from our thinking. Expecting to die, or expecting others to die, between ages of seventy and eighty years is a mind-set that predisposes us to less than what God declares we can have. There are probably a lot of grandpas and grandmas, great-grandpas and great-grandmas out there who would agree.

We have a biblical right to expect to live long and be effective for the kingdom of God should we so choose. Hopefully, we are making wise decisions now that affect our health in a positive manner, and that will also enable us to live a long life should we so desire. Let your desires be made known to your loved ones ahead of time should death come prematurely knocking at your door. Let them know whether you prefer to live or go on to be with the Lord if you were to die.

Settle it in your mind and spirit that we should not automatically dismiss the thought of praying for a deceased to be raised just because they may be seventy or eighty years of age. Get the mind of Christ and a sensing in your spirit on this issue. If the living loved ones expect you to pray for their older relative to be raised, then by all means, you should respond to their faith with yours, and not respond to what you see in the natural. Avoid the temptation to dismiss praying for a deceased just because they may be in their seventies and eighties.

On the other hand, the bodies of individuals do wear out and eventually elderly people desire to go home to be with the Lord. We should respect this fact. When this is the case, then so be it in considering this a plausible death. Release them and let them go in the peace and love of the Lord.

A LIFE OF HARDSHIP

We have established that just because a deceased may be seventy years or older does not mean that we should automatically dismiss praying for them to be raised. There is another corresponding mind-set to this one that should also be dispelled. Conversely, just because someone is young does not mean that we should automatically respond in praying for them to be raised. A life of hardship can be a valid reason for responding to a death as plausible.

Perhaps a deceased person lived a life full of hardship or pain and they would have no desire to stay on this earth and fulfill destiny any longer. We should respect the fact that a person gave up their will to live on this earth in exchange for eternal life when earthly circumstances became too overwhelming. A modern day example of this was shared with me by another individual and is used with her permission.

The call of God on her brother was recognized at a very early age. He preached his first sermon from his church's pulpit at the age of about nine or ten. By sixteen, he was licensed by his denomination, and ordained in it at eighteen. Then he allowed his life to veer off course, eventually leaving the ministry. He died at thirty-four. He definitely had not fulfilled the call of God on his life. His earthly destiny in God was as fulfilled to the degree that it was ever going to be. Yet, in the months before his death while his body began to succumb to disease, he returned to the Lord. Nonetheless, his life was in shambles.

Along with the disease, he faced relationship issues, financial problems, and legal charges. While he had returned his heart to the Lord and well knew the power of the Lord to heal him, health only meant having to deal with all of the other issues. He neither had the will, faith, or strength to press through all of those situations. It was easier for him to refuse life support and allow the disease in his body to take its course. He viewed death as his way of escape. He had set his will on that solution and on passing into eternity with the Lord.

Praying for this man's physical body would be praying against his will. While raising may have restored life, and possibly even his health, it would not have changed the other situations and he was not in a spiritual condition to walk (much less fight) through them. Restored health may have simply meant that he returned to his sinful lifestyle rather than going to heaven at this particular *time* to be with the Lord. It was his decision.

While it was not easy for his family to lose him, there was no indication here that they should fight to bring him back. In fact, he did not want it. Also, God had been faithful to answer his sister's desperate prayer many years earlier when she prayed, "God, whatever it takes, cause him to return to You." His sister's prayer indeed came to pass and she is fully persuaded that her brother is in heaven today. His life in this present world was over — finished, completed, as fulfilled as it would ever be.

As ministers, we may sense in our spirits that we are in a situation such as this, and the Spirit of the Lord is prompting us to bring this situation to a close. If so, we need to be sensitive to the emotional state and needs of the living loved ones. We will need to learn how to graciously bring these situations to a close if the deceased is not raised. As a wise suggestion, we should stay and comfort them during this time of grief, if at all possible, and not just pray with them.

DESTINY FULFILLED

We earlier stated that a plausible death comes into view when it can be realized that a person's destiny in God was as complete on earth as it was going to be. We may find ourselves coming into a situation and merely confirming this fact to the living loved ones. One biblical story involving a plausible death is recorded in Deuteronomy 34:4-7. This pertains to God's great servant, Moses, when he arrived at the promised land of Canaan.

God said to Moses, *"I have caused you to see it with your eyes, but you shall not cross over there."* The destiny of Moses was to lead the children of Israel to a land promised to them by God. Moses finally led them to this place, but could not cross over and go into this land. His earthly tasks were complete. Verses 5 and 6 inform us that Moses died right there in the valley of Moab.

The most poignant point of this story in regard to destiny was stated earlier in verse 7. *"Moses was one hundred and twenty years old when he died. His eyes were not dim, nor his natural vigor diminished."* God gave Moses what He had earlier promised, one hundred twenty years, and then took him while he was still healthy and strong. The earthly destiny of Moses was as fulfilled as it was ever going to be. He fulfilled the lifespan of one hundred twenty years that God promised mankind.

HEZEKIAH

Another interesting story relating to that of destiny being fulfilled is found in II Kings 20:1-6. This story has to do with a king named Hezekiah. II Kings 18:1-6 states that Hezekiah was twenty-five when he began to reign as king over Jerusalem, and He reigned for twenty-nine years. The Bible states that during the process of his reign, he did that which was right in the sight of the Lord. He held fast to the commandments of the Lord, and prospered wherever he went. And, most interesting, the bible states that there were no other kings, before or after, like him when it came to trusting in the Lord.

It came to pass that Hezekiah became very sick and near death. He was told by the Lord, through a prophet, to get his house in order because he was going to die. In other words, God told him that his earthly destiny was quickly coming to an end. Why God told Hezekiah that he was going to die, we do not know. God does not usually make a habit of telling someone when they are going to die. If God did, we might have a tendency to respond like Hezekiah and reap the same results.

Hezekiah turned his face toward the wall and prayed. He wept bitterly upon hearing that he was going to die. He outright refused to accept the fact that his death was going to be a plausible one.

Consequently, the word of the Lord came to him once again.

2 Kings 20:5-6 states, *"I have heard your prayer, I have seen your tears; surely I will heal you. And I will add to your days fifteen years."* God did indeed add fifteen years to Hezekiah's life. However, when you continue to follow his life from this time forth, he made one grave mistake that had a devastating and long lasting impact on the nation of Israel for several generations to come. He exposed the treasury of the house.

Hezekiah was then told in 2 Kings 20:17-18 that, *"Behold, the days are coming when all that is in your house, and what your fathers have accumulated until this day, shall be carried to Babylon; nothing shall be left,' says the Lord." And they shall take away some of your sons who will descend from you, whom you will beget; and they shall be eunuchs in the palace of the king of Babylon."*

Needless to say, it would have been better for Israel had Hezekiah accepted his death when God told him he was going to die. Likewise, we will have to learn and discern when and how to accept death as painful as it may be. This outcome is especially reflected in the next story.

SMITH AND POLLY WIGGLESWORTH

Another example of a story that required a bit more confirmation in coming to grips with a plausible death is seen in the modern day story of Smith Wigglesworth's wife, Polly. Wigglesworth and his wife were both evangelists of the early 1900s. According to the account, Smith was at the train station about to depart on a trip when he heard his wife had collapsed of a heart attack and died on her way home from the mission they founded.

"Rushing to her bedside, he found that her spirit had already departed to be with the Lord. Not settling for this, Smith immediately rebuked the death and her spirit came back, but only for just a short while. Then the Lord spoke: 'This is the time that I want to take her home to Myself.' So with a

breaking heart, Smith released his partner, the one he had loved for so many years, to be with the Lord. Polly Wigglesworth served the Lord until the very last moment of her life, January 1, 1913."[4]

Like the prior story involving life's hardships, we have to be ready and willing to release individuals to the spirit realm when God speaks to this end, even though it may pain us to do so. Like Polly Wigglesworth's, their destiny in this earth is as fulfilled as it is ever going to be.

APOSTLE PETER AND DORCAS

As we should be ready and willing to release deceased individuals to the spirit realm, we should also be ready and willing to pray them back. One such instance in the Bible is found in Acts 9:36-42. This story involves the Apostle Peter and a disciple named Dorcas. Verse 37 lets us know that she became sick and died. The prior verse lets us in on the fact that Dorcas *"was full of good works and charitable deeds."*

This statement could be construed in one of two ways by the living loved ones. Dorcas lived a good, full life and fulfilled destiny up until the time she died, therefore, her death could have been deemed plausible. On the other hand, the fact that she *"was full of good works and charitable deeds"* could be construed to mean that there was even more she could continue doing if raised. Evidently, the disciples responded with the latter viewpoint in mind.

These disciples sent two men to Apostle Peter and implored him to come quickly because Dorcas had died. We should stop and ask ourselves these questions: What went on in the minds of these disciples that made them call for Peter? Do you think that the disciples sent for Peter so he could come conduct a funeral? No. The disciples could have conducted a funeral themselves.

---

4. Roberts Liardon, *God's Generals* (Tulsa, OK: Albury Publishing, 1996), 210-211.

It becomes very clear to us when Peter arrived why the disciples sent for him to come. Peter came on the scene and responded with his faith to that of the disciples' faith. He did what was expected of him as an Apostle. He raised the dead. He cleared everyone out of the room from where Dorcas laid and began praying. He commanded life to come to the body of Dorcas. After he did this she opened her eyes and sat up.

This is one example of a situation where the individuals automatically kicked into a mode of faith rather quickly and summoned for Peter to come. They felt that Dorcas should not have died when she did, and they were right.

HIDDEN SIN AND GOD

As a word of wisdom, we must not always assume that just because a death *appears* to be premature to us that it may, in reality, be a plausible one. Our job is just to pray, exercise our faith and believe. The outcomes are best left in God's hands. For instance, a person's sudden death may be attributable to hidden sin that no one knows about.

Acts 5:1-11 is the story about two people named Ananias and Sapphira. Ananias and Sapphira sold a possession and then they were to take the money and lay it at the apostle's feet. They kept back a portion of the proceeds for themselves instead of laying all the money at the apostle's feet.

When they were confronted by the Apostles about this matter, they both lied instead of coming forward with the truth. In other words, Ananias and Sapphira misappropriated God's money and kept back a portion of it for themselves. As a result of their lying, the Holy Spirit simply removed the life out of their bodies and they dropped lifeless to the ground.

The point in bringing this story to light serves the purpose of providing us with an example of a plausible death that very well could have been perceived as premature by others on the outside of the situation. Given this situation, it is easy to see that we should not automatically assume that a death is premature just because it looks like it is premature. This is a prime example of why it helps to have our spiritual senses exercised to discern what is the will of the Holy Spirit in these situations.

The destiny of Ananias and Sapphira on this earth was as complete as it was going to get. It was evident to those on the inside why Ananias and Sapphira dropped dead. I believe I would be safe in assuming that I do not think any of the people inside this situation had faith arise in their spirits for the purpose of seeing these two individuals raised back to life.

At this point, I want to interject that there does indeed come a heightened awareness of the power of the Holy Spirit with regard to this apostolic dimension — whether to see life restored or removed.

The outcome of this story should not be construed to mean that the life of everyone who drops dead should be in question of hidden sin. This thinking would be absurd. The primary point being conveyed is that we might possibly pray for someone to be raised because we deemed their earthly death to be premature when, in fact, the Holy Spirit removed the life from the deceased.

This fact serves to remind us that we should learn to take the outcome of these situations in the same vein whether the deceased is raised or not. Recognize that it is our job to respond and react to the best of our spiritual abilities. The outcome will be up to God after this. After all, He is the Giver and Taker of life.

A RULE OF THUMB

Deaths will not always readily appear plausible or premature. The factors we discussed — pertaining to unbelievers, age, hardships and sin, not to mention many others — all reveal why we should refrain from quickly sizing up a death as plausible or premature. Our human reasoning can deceive us. In short, a plausible or premature death may not always be what it appears to be.

It is easy to see how the referenced factors, if not properly informed about such, could easily cause us to baulk in our decisions to enter into these situations. This fact serves the purpose of revealing that we should all the more do what Jesus did. We should abide by the rule of thumb to enter into these situations on the basis of what we sense in our spirit, and not on mere human reasoning. Again, our human reasoning can deceive us.

Additionally, understanding the nature of these factors reveal why it is so difficult to attach a point blank definition or criteria to premature death. The variables are wide in scope and ambiguous in nature. Perhaps God intended it this way. It forces us to rely on Him when finding ourselves drawn into death situations. God makes the ultimate decision about life being restored, not us. We are merely vessels through which He restores life if He so chooses when the necessary actions of faith are in operation.

PREPARATION NOW

Now that we have had some basic guidelines and fundamental insights illuminated for our understanding, we should begin to look at how we can naturally prepare for a premature death long before one ever happens. Death situations will present themselves to all of us and our families sooner or later. We can continue to prepare by further educating ourselves on this subject.

The question we should stop and ask ourselves is this: Will we be adequately prepared to respond and react with the necessary degree of faith, compassion and love to see a deceased raised if the situation elicits such a response? Time and further preparation will tell.

PART TWO:

PREPARING FOR A PREMATURE DEATH

While *Part One* dealt with establishing a spiritual foundation for moving in this dimension, *Part Two* addresses some of the natural and realistic aspects we might initially expect in preparing for this dimension. We will see that there is much more preparation that should be taking place now, long before someone dies. A sense for some of the mental constraints which have prevented us from entering into this dimension will also begin to be realized.

An awareness for the kind of unconventional actions that will possibly be associated with this dimension will be discussed. The permissibility of these actions will be illuminated as well. Also, the spiritual freedom and liberty to enter into these situations should begin to be realized.

My objective in presenting the following issues in this section is so the reader will begin to unearth their own natural and spiritual potential, not to mention confidence, to enter into these situations.

CHAPTER SIX

~

SHIFT YOUR THINKING

"...That I may know him and the power of His
resurrection... if, by any means, I may attain to
the resurrection from the dead."
Philippians 3:10-11

Natural preparation ahead of time is just as much to our advantage as spiritual preparation when it comes to raising the dead. The two will meet when a decision is made to enter into this dimension. But, how do we even begin to personally and practically prepare now for such a situation other than from the Word of God? The starting place usually begins right between our two ears — with our natural mind.

Our way of thinking determines our behavior. As we begin to deal with our mindset about this subject, hopefully our responses and reactions will gradually shift from a passive mode into a more

65

active one when someone dies. But first, it would be extremely helpful to understand the unconventional nature of the acts of faith that might possibly be required of us to raise the dead.

Let's take a look at these particular aspects in order to gain some further wisdom and insight for moving into these situations.

A MIND-SET SHIFT

On December 30, 2001, eleven days after receiving the word of the Lord about this book, I interjected a very small aspect of it into the message of a Sunday night service. I basically stated that, if we are going to be the powerful Church that raises the dead, then we have to be prepared to meet death. Little did I know that the next night would prove to be my first wake-up call.

My husband and I were in our first floor hotel room preparing to minister at a New Year's Eve service. Down the hall was the swimming pool and weight room. All kind of commotion was beginning to take place within the hotel in anticipation of the New Year's celebration. I was in the bathroom putting on my makeup when all of a sudden the loud sound of a metal door banging open against a cinder block wall resonated throughout the hallway. A blood-curdling scream at the same time of "someone call 9-1-1" echoed to the marrow of anyone's bones who heard it!

My husband quickly headed down the hall to see if there was anything he might do to help. In the meantime, I called the front desk to inform them what I had heard. I could only imagine that something dreadful had happened, and I was right. My husband arrived in the pool area to find people gathering around a lifeless little boy who had been pulled from the bottom of the pool. Blood was dribbling from his nose as his lifeless form lay at the side of the pool.

My husband looked among the crowd of people standing around this little boy's body. He and another woman began to reason among themselves that CPR could not hurt this child. They did this until the Emergency Medical Technicians (EMTs) arrived. Their efforts appeared futile in that the little boy simply was not responding. The EMTs arrived several minutes later and began to take over. Desperate attempts to resuscitate this little boy continued to appear futile.

This scene, however, is just one part of the emotional picture. We have to understand what was going on in the meantime with the mother in order to grasp my point for presenting this story. She had been escorted just outside of the pool area. While all the people were gathered at the poolside around this little boy, I was in my room and within ear-shot of the mother's reactions to what had just transpired. She was the emotional picture of what the devil expects when death tries to impose itself like a thief.

This mother was totally overcome with emotion that words cannot aptly describe. Uncontrollable grief had gripped the very depths of her being. As far as she was concerned, her little boy's life was over and she was responsible. She was wailing from her innermost being. I remember her exact words to be, "My baby! My baby! I just didn't see him. If I had just been watching..."

Her every thought and action indicated that God-breathed life could never be returned to the body of her little boy. This woman was the pure epitome of how the devil expects us to respond when death imposes itself on our situations — helpless and hopeless! This is the mind-set I am talking about confronting when someone dies.

The point I am trying to bring home is, we should immediately bring our every thought into captivity that points to the helpless, hopeless and pervasive attitude that an individual's life is unquestionably over when someone dies. In other words, we should get rid of that helpless and hopeless feeling and realize there may be another option. There are further steps of recourse.

Our experience involving this little boy proved to be an invaluable lesson where our thinking was concerned. It was easy to see how the dramatic and emotional elements surrounding a death can easily pervade our thinking, and resulting unbelief, if not carefully guarded. The events of the night jolted us into the reality of capturing the truth that there is another option even when situations look totally grim.

The best part of this story is that it *finally* ended on a good note. All of a sudden, the little boy started hacking and coughing up water, and started crying. When this happened, once again, the mother could hardly contain herself while the father put an unforgettable "bear hug" on my husband.

The devil wants believers to continue buying into this helpless and hopeless idea that death has to be accepted without recourse or question. This mind-set has pervaded the thinking of believers within the Body of Christ since the Dark Ages of the Church. The line of thinking in this regard is a flagrant lie straight from the pit of hell. The time has come for this mentality to begin changing.

We can begin changing right now by conditioning our mind and spirit to reflect the possibility of the fact that God-breathed life can be returned to an individual when someone dies; that is, if we learn to exercise the necessary kind of faith that might possibly be required.

UNCONVENTIONAL FAITH

The age-old term called *faith* has been handed down through the Church age, almost to the point of callousness. The tendency exists to skim right over this word and take for granted that we know what it means when it comes to raising the dead. However, we should not assume to have an in-depth understanding of the type of faith required to raise the dead until we can actually begin to recognize it.

Would we really recognize the kind of faith required for raising the dead if we saw it in action? Could this kind of faith possibly be offending? Could an unbeliever possibly be appalled if they saw this type of faith in action? The answer to all three questions is, yes!

Faith for raising the dead could come across as unconventional and out of order even to the most discerning individuals if not cognizant of this insight. We would be wise to go to the Scriptures for some understanding of this phrase, *unconventional faith*, in light of this fact.

WHEN JESUS SAW THEIR FAITH

One story that particularly demonstrates the principle of unconventional faith, even though it does not pertain to a death, is found in Mark 2:1-12. This passage of Scripture is the story of a paralytic man, and four other men, who helped carry him to a meeting that Jesus was conducting.

Jesus was preaching in a house in the city of Capernaum. The number of people gathered to hear Him teach was so large that there was no more room to receive anyone else inside the house. Upon realizing they could not enter this house in the *conventional way*, the faith of the paralytic man and his friends proved that *where there is a will, there is a way*.

These four men carried the paralytic up to the top of the house. The four men began tearing the roof off the top of the house once they got there. They tore a hole big enough to be able to lower the paralytic, bed and all, down into the house. This story is simply stated, but we have to understand what was really going on here in order to *see* the unconventional actions of faith at work.

First, the four men carried the paralytic up on the roof. Regardless of whether it was easy to get up on the roof or not, can we imagine walking by a house where four men are in the process of carrying a handicapped person on a bed up to a roof? Even if being on a rooftop was common for the houses of that day, notice what happened next.

The men not only managed to get the man up to the roof, but they began to tear up the roof. What would we think if we saw men tearing up a roof with a paralytic lying next to them? Even if it were a thatch-type roof where the fronds could easily be repositioned, there is a good possibility that debris was possibly falling into the house below. The commotion had to get the attention of all the people inside the house, including Jesus.

I wonder if Jesus had to calm down the owners of that home as their roof was being torn apart. What was their reaction to all of this commotion? What were they thinking at the audacity of these men? Perhaps everyone within the house was paralyzed with disbelief at what was happening right before their very eyes as the man was being lowered into the house.

Take a moment to think, in all honesty, of how we might have responded to this situation if we were the owner of the house. There is no way we would have let them tear a hole in our roof without asking questions. More than likely, I would have told them to get off my property or I would summon the proper authorities, if I had not already done so. Above all, I would not have wanted them to interrupt the meeting because I had guests in my home listening to the Master teach.

In the midst of all this commotion that these men created, verse 5 of Mark 2 states that, *"...when Jesus saw their faith."* Jesus called these destructive and intrusive actions, *faith.* Can we imagine the possible reaction on the faces of the people in that house when Jesus pronounced these unconventional acts to be faith!

Jesus turned to the paralytic man in Mark 2:11-12 and, after commenting on this type of faith, told him to take up his bed and walk. The man immediately obeyed the command of Jesus. The Bible states that all were amazed and glorified God. Verse 12 goes on to further state that the people said, *"We never saw anything like this!"*

UNDERSTANDING UNCONVENTIONAL FAITH

As we begin to understand and recognize what unconventional

faith may look like, we will better be able to see how seemingly inappropriate actions of faith might be perceived by others as conventionally out of order. These unconventional actions could very well be perceived as socially inappropriate, mentally questionable, and spiritually shortsighted. Behaviors associated with these descriptions may very well shock a given culture's societal expectations when it comes to raising the dead.

Whether in a church, funeral home, cemetery, house, or wherever we find ourselves, it is very possible that unconventional actions may have to be instigated if raising the dead becomes reality. Additionally, believers will need to be equipped to properly discern when unconventional actions to raise the dead are birthed and borne out of faith. For

> *Just because the reality exists that unconventional actions may be required to raise the dead, it should in no way be construed as an invitation to justify any and every unconventional behavior displayed.*

instance, we would not want to inappropriately interfere with another's faith by readily mistaking their unconventional actions as being out of order.

As a word of caution though, Christians should not merely act unconventional for the sake of being unconventional. This point cannot be emphasized strongly enough. Just because the reality exists that unconventional actions may be required to raise the dead, it should in no way be construed as an invitation to justify any and every unconventional behavior displayed. A real possibility exists for individuals to operate out of pure zeal if not careful in this regard.

The risk of the dead not being raised is a real likelihood until everyone involved. It should be understood that this type of faith may merit unconventional actions that are a spontaneous response to a naturally and spiritually unfolding situation, and *not something a believer forces to happen for the sake of being unconventional.*

CHARTING OUR TERRITORY

It goes without saying that Christians may have to exercise faith in an unconventional manner, to whatever degree, if raising the dead is to become a reality. For example, policies and procedures for handling deceased individuals are in place. They function like clockwork within hospitals, doctors' offices, hospices, emergency rooms, churches, funeral homes, etc. The author is presently unaware of any institutionalized policy or procedure that openly encourages individuals to come together for the purpose of raising the dead.

Such a policy or procedure probably does not exist because expectations for individuals to be raised from the dead have, for the most part, been virtually non-existent. Suffice it to say that, the real possibility exists that we might have to arrange for other options within these kinds of environments. The key factor here is that we remain open with our faith even when it looks dismal. We will have to keep making a way where there seems to be no way if we truly believe that a death is premature.

More than likely, we may have to come out from behind closed doors in order to command life to be returned to the deceased. For this reason, our territory will more than likely be charted under an unconventional label until the idea of Christians raising the dead becomes more commonplace, or should I say, conventional.

REPUTATION

We should not be too quick to assume that we presently possess the kind of faith required to raise the dead until we begin to comprehend the probable behaviors associated with this dimension.

comprehend the probable behaviors associated with this dimension. For example, would we be willing to exercise this type of faith in front of others who might perceive us to be totally out of order? Granted, the option of exercising faith in such an unconventional manner will, no doubt, be a risk to our reputation.

A risk to our reputation is one unavoidable risk we will have to take if moving into this dimension is to become a consideration. There's no way around this fact. Naturally speaking, no one in their right mind would want to deliberately risk bringing any type of reproach upon themselves. The bottom reality to this issue is that we will not be able to avoid this risk. It comes with the territory.

We might as well go ahead and get used to the idea of our reputation being challenged. As the Word of God becomes more established and settled in our spirit, the issue of reputation will become more of a peripheral one.

UNCONVENTIONAL RESULTS

There is no way to fully prepare individuals on how to begin entering into these situations. Conditioning our minds to see that death does not necessarily have to be over when someone dies is a good starting point. As we consider taking on more of an active approach into these situations, it helps to understand the term *faith* in light of the word *unconventional*.

We can safely conclude that we may have to approach conventional obstacles surrounding a death with unconventional faith. For the time being, this statement may be true until raising the dead once again becomes more of an integral part of Christian culture. In the meantime, unconventional faith will likely be accompanied by unconventional actions if unconventional results are to be realized.

CHAPTER SEVEN

~

A MODERN DAY
STORY

*"For as the body without the spirit is dead, so faith
without works is dead also."*

James 2:26

We discussed unconventional faith in the prior chapter, but let's
see how this type of faith may play out in a real life story. The story
we are going to examine is featured in a documentary entitled *Raised
From The Dead*. (See www.cfan.org.) It was produced by the ministry
of Reinhard Bonnke. You may or may not have already seen this story.
Even if you have, avoid the tendency to go ahead and skim over this
chapter.

This chapter will primarily focus on the actions of the believers
who were responsible for seeing that the deceased was raised. It will
not focus on the deceased individual. Instead, we will see how the
believers reacted and responded with their actions of faith, and how
these actions progressed into a very unconventional mode.

It is also important to note, for the sake of redundancy, that we will continue to allude to this story throughout the rest of this text. The reason for this is due to the documentary's validity and credibility. It is a resurrection story that, unlike many others, is well-documented with live video coverage, and is verified by all the secular and religious authorities that were involved in the situation. The author is unaware of another story as credible as this one.

The bottom line is that the resurrection power of the Holy Spirit is categorically irrefutable, but it took some bold, courageous and unconventional acts of faith from which we can learn.

A MODERN DAY STORY

This is an incredible story of unconventional faith that centers around a woman named Nneka Ekechukwu. She is the wife of a Nigerian pastor named Daniel. Pastor Daniel was involved in a fatal car accident. He was pronounced dead in two different hospitals by two different medical staffs. The last doctor to verify Pastor Daniel as dead signed and presented a death certificate confirming this fact.

Arrangements were made for Pastor Daniel's corpse to be transferred to a mortuary. Upon arrival at the mortuary, his body was embalmed, prepared for burial and placed in his casket; a fact also verified by the mortician. These facts set the stage for the real hero of faith, Nneka, to enter into the picture.

Nneka became emotionally distraught after watching her husband slowly die from the trauma of the accident. She was overcome with emotions of grief just like any ordinary person who suddenly lost a loved one. In fact, she became so emotionally distraught that she was told she needed to calm down, especially for the sake of her unborn child.

Nneka began to calm down as she and her children prepared to relocate to her father-in-law's home. It was during this time that Pastor Daniel's body was being prepared for burial. She had not even given serious consideration for Pastor Daniel to be raised before arriving at her father-in-law's.

Nneka began to regain her composure once she began to settle down for the night. Thoughts concerning Daniel's death began to unfold in her spirit during this time. She began to remember the prophetic word of the Lord that came to her prior to her husband's accidental death. This prophetic word was biblically based upon Isaiah 61.

The word to her was that she would not "experience any violation to her home again."[1] Thoughts concerning Daniel's death began to unfold in her spirit during this time. What we do know is that Pastor Daniel's death evidently fell within the scope of *another violation*. Whatever type of violation it was, God said it would not happen again, and Nneka began to hold God to His word.

This word of the Lord was the very premise and basis for what she needed to begin to fight a good fight of faith; and fight she did. She began to cry out to God in her father-in-law's house that first night, as she reminded Him of His prophetic word to her. She told God in her distress that this was another violation to her home, and that He had promised her she would not have another violation like this again.

The Apostle Paul states in 1 Timothy 1:18-19, *"according to the prophecies previously made concerning you, that by them you may wage the good warfare, having faith and a good conscience, which some having rejected, concerning the faith have suffered shipwreck."* In other words, we are to war with the prophecies that have gone over us so our faith will hold up and prophecies can be fulfilled. This meant that Nneka was going to have to wage some warfare.

---

1. Christ For All Nations; Reinhard Bonnke, *Raised From The Dead,* Documentary Video (Orlando, FL: Full Flame, LLC) February 2002.

As the prophetic word began to dawn on her that night, she said, "No, this cannot happen. I must do something to prove God again."[2] Faith for action began to stir in Nneka's spirit as she continued reminding God of her prophetic word. Evidently, the initial shock of Pastor Daniel's death only overtook her for a season. Actions would have to be taken in her grief stricken condition in order to keep her husband from going to an early grave. If she didn't, her faith was going to suffer *shipwreck*.

She immediately got up, went to her father-in-law during the night and woke him up. She requested permission from him to take Pastor Daniel's body to a city called Onitsha, where an evangelist by the name of Reinhard Bonnke was preaching. She believed the anointing would be so high there that this anointing would raise her husband. In other words, her husband being raised up at this particular place was the fundamental basis of her belief system that she needed to act upon.

Nneka's father-in-law considered her request and granted her permission for this to take place. This is the first main turning point in the story where progressive actions of faith began to take on a somewhat unconventional nature. Nneka was going to have to see to it that Pastor Daniel's body, currently at the morgue, was transported to Onitsha. Don't be too quick to overlook the ramifications of this statement.

This meant that Nneka and her father-in-law would have to approach the mortician to request that he let them remove Daniel's body and use his vehicle to transport it to Onitsha. This thought may be within the sphere of conventionality, but the purpose for which she was taking Daniel to Onitsha was not. She was taking him because she believed he could be raised from the dead.

---

2. Ibid.

Unconventionally speaking, could we imagine approaching a mortician with these thoughts after the body has already been embalmed and prepared for a funeral? The answer to this question is probably, no, by the majority. Nevertheless, the mortician conceded and helped plan the trip. In short, Nneka, her father-in-law and the mortician all left for Onitsha, a drive that would require approximately two hours of time.

Their going to Onitsha was a great idea. The only foreseeable issue at this point is that no one knew they were coming, and, no one knew who they were. They just unexpectedly showed up at the church grounds in the ambulance with a deceased. (An ambulance is also interchangeably referred to as a hearse in other cultures.)

They encountered the local security men who oversaw the comings and goings of the people at the church when they arrived. Nneka had to explain to the security men what was going on and why they were there. These men stated that it would be a great embarrassment to take a corpse inside the church building. They began to reason among themselves that if God wanted to perform a miracle for the deceased then the place really did not matter.

The place really did matter, as we have already established, in that this is the place where Nneka's faith rested for Daniel to be raised. Nneka would have to remain steadfast in the face of their rejection if Daniel was going to be ministered to at this place. Word of their arrival spread quickly, as the Nigerian State Security / Mobile Police Unit arrived on the scene shortly thereafter.

These men took Nneka's arrival serious. Unlike the local security men, the State Security demanded that the casket be opened to ensure that Nneka and her companions were not trying to smuggle a bomb into the church by telling the authorities that it was a dead person. This can be an understandable move in light of the culture but it was also an unconventional one.

Nneka's faith remained intact throughout this whole encounter as the police were inspecting the casket. These authorities saw that her motives were honest after inspecting the casket, but nevethless, the local security men told Nneka to take the casket and go away. Do you think that you would go away at this point and in the midst of taking unconventional actions such as these?

Nneka's faith would not let her leave. She began to cry and said to these men, "*I believe that he is going to come back to life! I believe!*"[3] This statement is the pinnacle and defining point of her faith that this author believes moved God. To understand this opinion, you really have to get the picture here.

Nneka is standing, looking unbelief squarely in the face — the local security men, local and state police, and others who had gathered by this time — and is still telling them that she *believes*. She stood firm and reiterated that her deceased husband was going to come back to life again if he was allowed to be prayed for under the anointing of these particular meetings.

Carefully take note of how God began to turn the tide in her favor after Nneka made this statement in the face of unbelief. Her infectious statement of faith persuaded some of the security men to start believing with her. They began to agree with her belief that God could raise this man. However, there were the other security men who remained steadfast in their stance of unbelief.

The momentum of belief that had shifted to the men who chose to believe was obvious by their actions. They literally began wrestling with the other unbelieving men over what should be done with the casket. The believing men started pushing the casket down toward the church while the opposing men would push it back. They were literally pushing the casket back and forth. Now they were arguing among themselves about whether the body should stay or go.

---

3. Ibid.

In the meantime, the pastor's son had recieved word of what was taking place at the gates of the church. He arrived on the scene at about this time. The pastor's son had the authority to make the final decision in this matter. He decided in favor of Nneka. He then gave wise instructions for how Daniel was to be taken into the church.

He stated that Daniel's body needed to be removed from the casket before taking it into the church. This was so the children would not be scared. Accordingly, the men took Daniel's body out of the casket and carried it down to the basement of the church. They laid it on two tables that had been pulled together.

Imagine the trying of Nneka's faith as the men were wrestling over her husband's casket. All these conventional obstacles had to be overcome just to get the body to this church in Onitsha, where her faith rested. All of this warfare had taken place and the body had not even been ministered to yet! Let these unconventional actions, that were taken directly in the face of adversity, be an insightful lesson to us.

Our unconventional actions of faith may very well be tested with what unbelieving believers or other unbelievers may think. Remember, faith is not faith if it wavers before God in front of unbelieving believers and other unbelievers, regardless of who they are or what authority they may carry.

MINISTERING TO DANIEL

Once Nneka went into the basement of the church where they laid Daniel's body, Nneka withdrew herself from the immediacy of the situation. She took a seat on the other side of the room where she could observe the individuals ministering to Daniel. Her responsibilities and authority had now been relinquished to the pastor's son.

The pastor's son evidently arranged for a couple of deliverance ministers at the church to come downstairs and minister life to

Daniel's body. They began drawing on the power of the Holy Spirit by speaking the Word of God to him and singing praises. Daniel did not respond immediately so they incorporated a more hands-on approach as time went on.

The ministers reasoned among themselves that the body had become very stiff due to the effects of the embalming fluids and by being in the casket. They felt they should begin massaging the muscles of his stiff body for these reasons. They started with Daniel's hands and arms and, little by little, the body started loosening and warming up. They continued by massaging and turning his neck. (Have you ever wondered why it is called *the working of miracles* in 1 Corinthians 12:10? Sometimes a miracle requires a little work!)

The most fascinating part of this story takes place as the ministers started rubbing the stiffness out of Pastor Daniel's body. The video camera zeroes in on Pastor Daniel's stomach area and visibly captures the point in time when abdominal breathing movements became visible to the human eye. There was no denying that the power of the Holy Spirit was restoring life to Daniel's body once again.

It became obvious after a period of time that life had returned to Daniel's body when he suddenly jumped off the table. His soul and spirit had reconnected with his physical body! We should remember that this was a man who died of internal and external injuries from a fatal car accident three days earlier. His blood stream had been injected with embalming fluids. His stiff body had been in a casket and prepared for burial for quite some time. Yet, he suddenly *jumped* off the table!

It became very plain to the natural eye that Daniel's body had been made whole. He was able to jump off the table because, one, a whole new blood supply had miraculously been superimposed over the embalming fluids. And two, all of the internal and external injuries that contributed to his death were gone. God totally restored his life back to him with a body that was, in the process, made whole.

This is what can happen when believers dare to become willing to set aside their reputation to steadfastly and wisely exercise unconventional faith expecting to see a deceased raised back to an earthly life, fully healed.

OBSERVATIONS AND INSIGHTS

This story is one that best demonstrates a compelling example of what is meant by exercising unconventional faith. No doubt, it is rich and overflowing with morsels of insight and wisdom! In light of the unconventional aspects associated with this dimension, there are many observations and insights that are worth noting from the story. The following are just a few.

Overall, we could see that Nneka's faith was an ongoing process that had to be steadfastly walked out. She had to continue walking it out even when it meant crossing over thresholds that required actions not so conventional. There was no backing out when it came to standing in the face of conventional adversity.

Another morsel of insight and wisdom worth noting is, we should never let unbelief overtake our spirit through our emotions and convince us that a deceased cannot return from the spirit realm. Initial and overwhelming emotions of grief are not necessarily a sign of unbelief as much as they are a natural response to a much needed release. Nneka was emotionally distraught but she repositioned herself under her father-in-law's authority and comfort. She began to calm down and think more clearly when she did this.

Nneka began to regain her composure, and remember God's prophetic word to her at this time. This is when faith began to rise and she came up with a plan of action. The sad part of Nneka's story is that she had no other believers to help her. This fact alone should make believers more keenly aware of the uphill battle we face until believers become more educated on this subject.

Hopefully, we will not find ourselves having to jump the hurdles Nneka did just to get capable and willing ministers to join their faith with ours in order to minister to our deceased loved one. Ideally, we will begin to be encircled by them.

The most vitally important point of wisdom and insight that is worth noting by this author is seen in how Nneka responded to her human opposition at the most critical time. The critical time is when it looks as if our unconventional actions of faith could teeter either way in a given moment. She continued responding with her statement of belief every time the *authorities* told her to go away. The situation began to completely turn around after she made convincing statements of faith to her human opposition at the peek and height of her adversity.

The last insight worth mentioning pertains to how Nneka reacted when she finally received some help from the ministers. She went into the basement and took a seat. Enormous relief from the battle had to be her portion at this point. She allowed the ministers to take over tending to Daniel's body as she distanced herself from the situation by taking a seat on the other side of the room. The situation changed for good even more when others were allowed to take charge of the ministry time.[4]

BETTER EQUIPPED

Many other valuable inferences can be drawn from this situation. These are just a few. The author strongly suggests obtaining a copy of

---

4. One mistake commonly made in Christian circles is that everyone prays and no one is *in charge* of the prayer time. Since the spirit world understands and recognizes authority, this charismatic chaos has often led to less than effective prayer times, whether for general intercession, deliverance, or whatever the purpose. Understand who is going to be commanding the deceased to be raised back to life and that all others are there to agree with and support that command.

this video for the many contributions it offers this field of study. This is but one case. There will be others to come as we learn to capture these experiences when they are happening. They will indeed aid the Body of Christ in our ongoing efforts to continually prepare for this dimension.

We may not necessarily know what is going to be involved in one of these situations; however, we should now be better equipped to recognize when unconventional actions are being exercised at a faith driven pivotal moment, and not confuse them with insanity.

CHAPTER EIGHT

~

DECISIONS TO INTERVENE

*"Behold, I give you the authority to trample on
serpents and scorpions, and over all the power of
the enemy, and nothing shall by any means hurt
you."*

Luke 10:19

Death happens to people we know and people we may not know.
A death may occur close to where we live or it may happen far away.
We may be able to do something about the death or we may not.
Sometimes we can see a death coming, while at other times the death
may be accidental. A mixed combination of such factors, not to
mention the environment, make for some interesting circumstances
in which we may find ourselves in these situations.

For example, we may find ourselves with:

    1) a deceased we know whose burial may not be planned;

2) a deceased we may not have known whose burial is planned;

3) a deceased we know and whose accidental death has just happened; or,

4) a deceased we do not know and whose death has just happened.

There are many other hypothetical combinations, but none of them affect what the Holy Spirit of God can do to raise a deceased. These factors will, however, shape some of the relational dynamics among believers and unbelievers who may find themselves together in one of these situations. This becomes important if faith is going to be exercised to see the deceased raised.

While we may not know exactly how we would respond in a death situation without the given set of circumstances and environment in which we would find ourselves, there are some varying constants worth mentioning for the sake of continued preparation. They are:

1) accepting responsibility for our actions

2) acting in a timely manner

3) the issue of embalming

4) confronting unbelief

Regardless of the emotional state someone may find themselves in, the following are issues that should be considered from the outset. Let's take a look at these issues as if we were going to enter in to one of these situations.

ACCEPTING RESPONSIBILITY

This first and foreseeable issue has to do with that of taking responsibility for our actions. Individuals who involve themselves in these situations should be willing to accept responsibility for their actions. This is especially true when the outcome is not what had been hoped. This point cannot be stressed enough!

These situations may not always turn out as we desire. Given this fact, outside influences need to keep a low profile and take a wait-and-see approach. Attempts to verbally coax, persuade, or influence another to exercise a right of recourse could be considered out of order. Individuals should not be unduly prodded to enter into one of these situations.

> ...decisions to intervene may be better off left in the hands of those who have the authority to initiate action.

The willingness to show full support after a believer steps forward in this dimension could then be deemed more appropriate. Individuals will have to live with the decision they make, after the fact. Any outside influences would want to avoid being on the receiving end of a possible and emotional backlash of blame, guilt, or hurt should the outcome not be favorable.

As a general rule of thumb, decisions to intervene may be better off left in the hands of those who have the authority to initiate action.

TIME

When we make a decision to enter into these situations, we should consider coming forth in a timely manner. This is especially true when you find yourself coming upon the seen of an accident where someone has just been killed. On the other hand, the time limits are pretty well defined when it comes to a burial or a funeral. Either way, time is an issue.

If we find ourselves coming upon the scene of an accident where someone has just died and we do not know the deceased, we may only have a small window of opportunity to step forward to intervene. Situations like this reveal the need for believers to be instant in and out of season with their faith. Otherwise, we may not see the deceased again and the window may close very quickly.

The window of opportunity to address the spirit of a deceased when a funeral or a burial may be planned is quite different. The circumstances and surroundings may not be quite as intense and pressing as those surrounding the scene of an accident. Either way, there is still a time issue to consider. We have more of a feel for how much time we have, in order to make a decision to step out in faith, when a funeral is imminent. Ideally, we will not let the deceased be lowered into the ground and covered, or cremated before we step out, or else, the possibility increases that we might find ourselves on our own after this.

Another reason time begins to be a consideration has to do with established laws governing a corpse in a given geographical region. These laws vary from region to region, but there are usually policies and procedures in place for the riddance of a corpse, especially if the deceased is not embalmed. We may find ourselves in the position of needing to exercise our faith before legally imposed time frames like this begin to encroach upon our territory.

This time factor will then begin playing even more of an integral part in our considerations to move forward. These legal time constraints are imposed upon us for good reason. One reason they were implemented was to avoid the spread of disease that can happen among decomposing bodies. With this in mind, we should endeavor to abide by the laws of the land.

It is for the good of other individuals that we make a decision to initiate action long before it gets to a questionable point if at all possible. This time issue also relates to the next consideration; that of embalming.

EMBALMING

Embalming is a procedure whereby a corpse is injected with a preservative in the form of a fluid. The purpose for embalming a deceased is to slow down the decomposing process so the body can temporarily be preserved a little longer. It has been the author's observation that one of the biggest barriers initially preventing Christians from entering in to raise the dead is attributable to the issue of embalming.

There is a tendency for believers to automatically overlook praying for a deceased if they have been embalmed. Many automatically believe that if a deceased is, or has been embalmed, that they cannot be raised from the dead. Simply stated, there is a pervasive stronghold of unbelief in the Body of Christ when it comes to the issue of embalming.

If this stronghold of unbelief is what we choose to believe, then this is what will come to pass. But, we do not have to believe this way. Not only can deceased individuals be raised after being embalmed, but embalming can also work for us as well.

Take, for instance, the story of Nneka and Pastor Daniel once again. We do know for a proven and well documented fact that Pastor Daniel's body was embalmed by a mortician. This procedure worked to his advantage in several ways. First, it provided Nneka with the necessary time to drive to the church in Onitsha and do what needed to be done.

A real possibility exists that this story may have rendered different results if Pastor Daniel's body had not been embalmed. For instance, do you think the pastor's son would have given instruction for Daniel's body to be removed from the coffin had it stank? Possibly not. Even if he did, it is probable that the men of the church would not have wanted to go near, or even be handling, the body.

Further, would the pastor have allowed the body to be carried into the basement of the church? Let's face it. Humans, some more than others, will only digest so much in the presence of a stinking corpse before backing off. Even Jesus was keenly aware of this fact.

He probably did not want to be near the offensive odor any more than you or I would. This insight is revealed in the story of Lazarus.

His directive to have the stone rolled away from the grave was so Lazarus could "come forth," not so He could go in. Jesus spoke these famous words of faith from a distance, and probably for good reason!

Why let a corpse get to a more advanced stage of decomposition in this day and time if it can be prevented? It is plain to see that embalming can serve to work to our advantage if we will let it. Our efforts to mobilize for ministry the way we need may require a little extra time. Embalming provides for the needed time.

On the other hand, we may find ourselves in the same situation as that of Nneka. Our deceased loved one may already be embalmed before we arrive at a decision to exercise our faith for their life to be restored. This is still no problem for God. Our preoccupation should be with an actionable plan of faith rather than worrying about whether our deceased loved one is embalmed.

Our humanly perceived limitations should not be confused as being an obstacle to God when it comes to embalming. Embalming can be a blessing in disguise instead of a justification for unbelief. It can be used as a stepping stone of faith instead of a stumbling block of unbelief. Jesus stated in Mark 9:23 that, *"if you can believe, all things are possible to him who believes."* This Scripture can be interpreted to mean that God can raise the dead even when embalming fluids are present in the body.

On a final note, let's think about the embalming process from one more perspective. When God raises an individual who has been embalmed, a whole new blood system will be supernaturally imposed upon the whole body. In light of this fact, there can only be more glory given to God when someone is raised from the dead who has been embalmed.

CONFRONTING UNBELIEF

We may have no other choice but to confront those close to us and others when it comes to unbelief. For purposes of this writing, the word "confrontation" should infer the ability to wisely address all manner of overriding unbelief in a firm and immovable manner without engaging in conflict. When confronting, we should work toward developing the ability to stay our course in the process without being offended and sidetracked. This is especially true when it comes to addressing unbelief by the various channels through which it may come and how it might manifest, be it service personnel or family members.

For instance, unbelief could manifest through service personnel who become involved in administrating matters pertaining to the deceased. A good example of this is the unbelieving believers Nneka encountered upon her arrival at the grounds of the church. Regardless of how unbelief surfaces, it may wisely need to be addressed by those in authority if it has the imminent potential to interfere with efforts to see a deceased raised.

Addressing unbelief may not always be a pleasant experience. Once again, we can look to Jesus for some insight into this statement. He encountered some interesting individuals when He arrived at the house of Jairus to attend to the daughter. He "*saw the flute players and the noisy crowd wailing*" when He arrived (Matthew 9:23-24).

People had already begun to gather and mourn the little girl's death. Chances are, some of these individuals were grieving family members. Jesus walked in and said to them in the midst of their grief, "*Make room, for the girl is not dead, but sleeping.*" Watch what happens when Jesus made this unconventional statement. The Bible says, "*And they ridiculed Him.*"

Other versions of the Bible state that the noisy crowd "*laughed him to scorn*" and "*scoffed and sneered.*" With this in mind, would we possibly be ready to be laughed at and sneered at to our face? Could we withstand scorn and ridicule from others for believing that we can command life to return to a deceased? Only when Christians are full of the Word of God about this subject will they be able to withstand this type of adversity with grace. In the meantime, living loved lones should give some consideration as to how to handle these potentially awkward situations.

Living loved ones should think about this story when extending an invitation for other believers to come on the scene and take charge. We will need to support these believers and their decisions to move forward in spite of how other family members or close individuals may feel about raising the dead. This may not be easy, especially if a particularly close relative is opposing you.

Christians are provided the referenced passage of Scripture involving Jesus, probably for good reason. If individuals acted inappropriately toward Jesus, Christians in this day and time may not escape this same reaction in their endeavors either. Living loved ones would be wise to prepare to respond accordingly if a similar situation arises, especially if family and friends do not share common beliefs about the dead being raised.

A living loved one, as well as another believer coming into the picture, should not be oblivious to the possibility of such resistance. Actions of faith could prove futile by the inappropirate behavior of unbelieving individuals who may try to cause faith to waver in these situations. We should be prepared to accommodate the minister we call upon the scene, and back up their directives.

Jesus tolerated the ridicule and scorn long enough to see what needed to be done. Matthew 9:25 gives a little insight as to what happened next by the statement "*when the crowd was put outside.*" Someone (probably Jairus since he was the head of the house) saw to it that these unbelievers were removed from the house so Jesus could do what needed to be done.

Apostle Peter had to do the same thing when he arrived to minister life to Dorcas. Acts 9:39 states:

"When he (Peter) had come, they brought him to the upper room. And all the widows stood by him weeping, showing the tunics and garments which Dorcas had made while she was with them."

Peter assessed this situation long enough to know what he had to do. Acts 9:40 states that *"Peter put them all out, and knelt down and prayed."* This time Peter put all the individuals out, and the disciples permitted this action. Peter's intentions were not to be insensitive or ugly to these grieving individuals. His intention was to create more of an atmosphere of faith in order to achieve the desired results.

We can only surmise how offended the people in both of these instances may have felt when this happened. Think about it. They were gathered together in their respective environments to offer their sincere and genuine condolences. All of a sudden they find themselves put out. It is easy to see how this unconventional action could easily be mistaken as offensive behavior toward the living loved ones for allowing this to happen.

Our focus, however, should not become the offense of others in these situations. It should be the resurrection of the deceased. Believers cannot afford to shy away from taking these actions if deemed necessary. We should prepare to wisely exercise our authority and confront these situations where an atmosphere of impeding and overriding unbelief interferes with ministering to a deceased. The possibility of this happening should not be discounted, particularly among families whose beliefs vary on this subject.

Remember, our obligation as a believer is to bring the faith of others up to another level. It is not to let the unbelief of others pull our belief down and overshadow our actions of faith. Focused faith for raising the dead will have to remain central in our approach. The more we encounter and experience death situations that require us to address issues of unbelief in this manner, the more mature we will become in seeing that the environment is subdued and mobilized.

Our foremost goal when we find ourselves in one of these situations should be to help create an infectious atmosphere of faith and lay the groundwork for what is to come.

GIVE SOME FORETHOUGHT

All these areas of consideration should provide for some interesting forethought in preparing to enter into this dimension. Living loved ones may have their work cut out in requesting for someone to come minister resurrection life to their deceased loved one. This fact will prove to be interesting if the minister is not the pastor or leader overseeing the affairs.Other considerations and dynamics such as this will begin to open up once we turn our thoughts in this direction. This is all a part of the preparation process.

One main dynamic that is sure to become a priority in our pre-considerations is that of having other like-minded believers surround us during these times. We should not have to exercise our faith alone if we can help it.

~

CHAPTER NINE

APPROACHING A DEATH

"He has made us competent as ministers of a new covenant."

2 Corinthians 3:6

Have you ever just stopped and thought about how you would respond if you found yourself facing the premature death of a particular loved one? Ideally, you should not have to approach the death alone, and without some good support. The previous chapter, *Decisions To Intervene,* began to incorporate the natural progression of other believers coming into the picture. These individuals will be referred to as *outside believers.*

The specific reason for outside believers coming into the picture is to assist, or, like Jesus, assume responsibility for seeing that the deceased is raised. We'll explore from the Bible what could be expected from these outside believers in the way of actions. Assuming they are willing to come in and assist, will they be granted the scope of authority to take the necessary steps of actionable faith for seeing that a deceased is raised?

We should first discuss some of the aspects of what this may entail in order to satisfactorily answer this question. We will see that living loved ones run the risk of tying the hands of outside believers if genuine efforts are not made to understand where they may be coming from in their ministry to the deceased. Exploring this subject with this issue in mind further serves one more basic and important purpose.

It will serve to further reveal if everyone involved might truly be prepared to, not only approach death, but mobilize and stick with the situation until the deceased is raised. Time, experience, and maturity will tell. In the meantime, let's take a brief look at the issues of authority and relationship. This will be essential in order to lay a little more groundwork before discussing what we could expect from an outside believer.

AUTHORITY AND RELATIONSHIP

We cannot be too quick to assume that just because we have been requested to come on the scene of a deceased that a broad scope of authority will be relinquished to us. We might possibly have our work cut out for us. This is especially true, for instance, where an outside believer may be called upon by a very close friend of the family. The close friend may know more about what an outside believer may need to do than the living loved ones.

Another instance where a broad scope of authority may not be granted to outside believers is where living loved ones only have very little understanding about raising the dead, except for the fact that it can be done. We will have to wade into these situations and minister to the best of our present abilities and to the fullest extent possible. This is all we can do.

Ideally, we would be requested to come pray for the deceased by the person with the authority to make decisions on behalf of the deceased. Realistically, situations are not presented to us in an ideal fashion. Having said this, it would be wise for us to enter into these situations and first ascertain the person responsible for making the bottom line decisions over the deceased.

Exception may be given to this fact if we find ourselves coming on the scene of an accident where someone was killed or where someone had dropped dead. We may have to assume the authority and take over in these instances. Otherwise, if living loved ones already know and have confidence in us, like Mary and Martha had in Jesus, we may already have the freedom and liberty to approach the deceased as we see fit.

Generally speaking, we would be wise to respectfully approach those in authority. Respect their decisions and minister to the extent that they will allow.

MOBILIZING

The only way to gain experience and maturity is to begin mobilizing to take action. Let's take a look at how these situations can unfold and what could take place. Hopefully, the following will aid us in approaching a seemingly premature death. We will do this by addressing three main questions in this and the next two chapters:

1. When is it permissible to intervene?
2. Who should or could be present?
3. How long should we stay?

WHEN IS IT PERMISSIBLE TO INTERVENE?

Obviously, the most opportune time to intervene in a death situation is right after an individual dies. Many people have earnestly prayed for their deceased loved one to be resurrected right at this time but to no avail. Perhaps this is why we do not think to move past this point. The situation all seems so final when ministry to the deceased is not fruitful at this time.

This is the crucial and pivotal point that we must zero in on, in order to change our conventional way of thinking. The majority of us would resign, give in and accept the outcome as *fate* or *the will of God* because the desired result was not obtained *when* ministry to the deceased first took place. God can again meet us in a different way if we will remain open for other options and are willing to continue pressing into the situation.

If further intervention sounds preposterous, we should brace ourselves to move to another place in God. This is where these situations will begin to turn unconventional. As we will see, solid scriptural support exists for further intervention from the outset, before, during or after a funeral.

INTERVENING RIGHT AFTER A DEATH

2 Kings 4:8-37 is the story of a Shunnamite woman whose young son unexpectedly died. He died in her arms shortly after a servant had brought him in from her husband's field. In her grief, she carried her son's body to an upstairs chamber in her house and laid him on the bed. She went out of the room and shut the door behind her. She told *no one* of her son's death — a difficult thing to do.

She then requested of her husband that she be allowed to go see a prophet of God named Elisha. Her husband asked her, *"Why?"* She could have told him that their son was dead. Instead, she answered him by replying, *"It is well."* Her husband had a donkey saddled for her, and then she headed straight for Elisha's house. It is extremely important to take note of this story at this point in that it can very well relate to us today.

Take note that this woman's belief system first took her straight to the prophet Elisha; not a funeral director. Consider the following thought for a moment, as hard as it may be to our natural way of thinking. If we truly believe from the outset that a loved one will be raised, should a funeral even be planned? In other words, does this sound like having a Plan B — a funeral in place if Plan A — resurrection ministry did not work? You decide.

This is not to say that we should not plan a funeral, especially if our faith has not yet reached this level of maturity. If the death of an individual comes over an extended period, and much prayer had taken place during this time of sickness, it might seem pointless for the living loved ones to allow further ministry to take place. But, if another opportunity arose through other outside believers who came upon the scene, we should still remain open in our faith.

Whatever decision we make, it should be borne out of our present level of faith and not that of another's. Decisions of faith will also be those that begin to dawn on us in the process of walking out the situation and where we find ourselves. We may have no other choice but to start with a funeral home if that is where the deceased has already been taken and prepared.

The Shunnamite woman's son died at home, and she chose another option. She did not have his body prepared for a burial. Instead, she headed straight for a prophet with whom she and her husband already had an existing relationship. No unbelieving individuals had to be addressed. She used wisdom to keep the unbelief at bay and away from her dwelling so Elisha could do what a prophet is expected to do — command life to enter the child's body once again.

The child arose after a good fight of faith by Elisha.

INTERVENTION BEFORE A FUNERAL

We can still intervene even if a deceased's body has been prepared for burial. Again, we should briefly reflect back on the story of Jairus as evidence of intervening from the outset of a funeral. As we discussed earlier, other individuals had already begun to congregate at the ruler's home. A conventional scenario of grieving individuals and funeral music had already unfolded by the time Jesus arrived.

Jesus obviously had no second thoughts about mobilizing the environment to approach death even though the girl's body was to be prepared for burial. His intention was to walk into that house and command life to return to the little girl's body. This is exactly what Jesus did and that is exactly what happened — before any funeral process started unfolding.

Again, intervening at this stage may be a typical response for many who have attempted to minister life to a deceased *one last time* before the funeral started. From a scriptural standpoint, the battle still does not have to be over if we are willing to cross conventional thresholds even more and step forward.

INTERVENTION IN THE MIDDLE OF A FUNERAL

There is also occasion in the Bible where intervention to restore life to a deceased took place in the middle of a funeral procession. This is another story we have already addressed, but we did not address it from this perspective. It is the story involving the deceased son of the widow at Nain, in Luke 7:11-17.

This passage of Scripture informs us that the widow's son was being carried out of the gate of the city as Jesus was going in. Jesus stepped forward in the middle of the procession and spoke up as the young man was being carried out. Everything came to a standstill when this happened. He told the grieving widow not to cry. He then gave a command for the son to arise. You know the rest of the story — the young man sat up and began talking in his coffin.

Would this kind of behavior be deemed unconventional by the vast majority of unbelievers, not to mention believers, today? It probably would. This is probably why we have not followed through with actions of faith to this degree, much less thought about it. It is one of those unthinkable and unspoken societal barriers. Nonetheless, Jesus' unconventional action in this story, which came at a faith-driven pivotal moment, contributed to the raising of this man.

One modern day conclusion we can draw from this story is apparent. Just because a body is en route to be buried does not mean that the opportunity for the deceased to be raised is over. It is not over until actions of faith have been exhausted by the believers doing the ministering.

Even if efforts to intervene in the middle of the funeral prove futile, the further possibility of intervening should not be ruled out.

INTERVENTION AT THE END OF A FUNERAL

It would be wise to remind you what Jesus said before discussing this next option. Jesus said that believers *shall do greater* than He did. One merely has to take a look at the story of Lazarus from another angle for the full realization to dawn on us that we have the God-given, biblical right to remain open for intervention after a funeral (John 11:1-44).

We know that Lazarus had already been placed in his grave before Jesus arrived. Everything was over except the crying, when Jesus arrived on the scene. Jesus requested that Martha and Mary take Him to the cave where Lazarus was buried. He gave a directive for the stone to be rolled away from the grave and commanded Lazarus to come forth.

As you well know, Lazarus came forth out of his grave after the funeral was over and after he had been put in his final resting place. I would be remiss if I disregarded addressing the reality of intervening with this option in mind. In order for many of us to go back to a grave and open it after someone has been buried is illegal. This action is commonly referred to as grave digging. Grave digging is especially illegal in Western cultures.

Please take note that the author is not advocating grave digging. Opening a grave is not an action that we should just arbitrarily take just because we know that Jesus had it done. As a word of admonition, we would be well advised to remember that actions to intervene at this time should be ones that are generated from a sensing of the Holy Spirit and strictly at a *faith-driven and pivotal moment*.

If grave digging is not illegal or closely supervised then there is nothing to stop us other than unbelief. But, if we know grave digging to be illegal then we would be wise to exercise actions of faith before this time. Otherwise, we may find ourselves having to act alone. If grave digging is not illegal where you reside, and an outside believer comes along like Jesus did after the deceased has been buried, then so be the end result according to your actions of faith.

Again, it should be reiterated that such actions should be borne out of a *faith-driven and pivotal moment*.

DECENCY AND ORDER

Ministering life to a deceased is unconventional in itself for the time being. This fact does not even take into consideration the permissibility of intervening before, during, or after a funeral. These ideas will take some getting used to in the Body of Christ. Yet, these times of intervention are the examples Jesus left for us. His example leads us back to the issue posed earlier.

Would we, as a living loved one, grant an outside believer the authority to intervene during these various times if the situation called for such? Moreover, would we be willing to step forward right before, during, or after a funeral to minister to a deceased? Jesus was willing, and therefore, so should we as we mature along the way.

On the other hand, the Bible states that we should let all things be done decently and in order (I Corinthians 14:40). But, before decency and orderliness is established, the Bible says to let all things be done. With regard to the subject at hand, the Church will experience growing pains in establishing for decency and order until raising the dead becomes a conventional and accepted order of business within the Church. In the meantime, we will have to give ourselves, and others, the grace to grow in walking out these situations.

Intervening in the middle of a funeral, or after one is over, like Jesus did, does not naturally come across as being in order. However, we should remember that Jesus was establishing the Church and implementing church doctrine as He walked this earth. Just because He raised the dead during and after a funeral should not be construed to mean that this should become the norm. Ideally, Christian believers will learn how to wisely approach and address these situations from the outset of a funeral. Hopefully, closure can be achieved then by the loved ones - either way. If it is not, further intervention should not be ruled out.

To this end, we should answer the first major question posed earlier in this chapter. When is it permissible to intervene in a death situation? It is permissible to intervene at any point in time that spontaneous actions of faith are forthcoming — whether at the beginning, middle or end of a funeral.

CHAPTER TEN

~

THE PRESENCE OF OTHERS

"Thou shalt also decree a thing, and it shall be established unto thee: and the light shall shine upon thy ways."

Job 22:28

We will not always be able to control the atmosphere and environment when ministering to a deceased. We can, however, create a more conducive one when it is within our authority, discretion and ability to do so. This is particularly true when it comes to the presence of other people being present and the time comes to minister to the deceased. This issue leads us to the second major question we posed in the previous chapter: Who could be present in one of these situations?

The presence of other individuals being privy to our actions in raising the dead is a natural concern to many believers. Perhaps this is why we may feel the need to skirt around others in order to minister to a deceased. This secrecy of this dynamic will gradually begin to shift the more this subject becomes integrated into Christian culture. In the meantime, we can begin to gain some insight from the Bible on how to address this issue before approaching one of these situations.

As with the prior issue of *when to pray*, there are no given set of rules. We do, however, have the example of Jesus as our guide in this regard. The presence of others could very well be a matter of the living loved ones' desire. An outside believer's personal preference and spiritual maturity could also factor into the picture. Then again, we may have no other choice but to outright step forward especially if we find ourselves coming upon the scene of an accident, or where someone has dropped dead.

Seeing how the Bible is the most credible place to resort to for some insight on this issue, let's continue looking there. We will observe how three particular scenarios played out with this issue in mind. They are when a believer:

1) ministers life to a deceased when requested to come into the situation, and without the presence of others;
2) ministers life to a deceased when requested to come into the situation, but in the presence of others; and
3) ministers life to a deceased when not requested to come into the situation, and in the presence of unbelievers and believers.

By and large, we would not want to limit God because of where we may find ourselves positioned among other individuals when death crosses our path.

MINISTERING TO THE DECEASED ALONE

The story of Dorcas in Acts 9:36-42 well depicts Peter's preference to enter into the room alone to minister to Dorcas. We know that he was summoned by the disciples to come because Dorcas died. He arrived at the upper chamber where Dorcas had been laid. Weeping women were also there grieving her death. Peter had them "*all*" put out of the room if you will remember. Not even the disciples who called him to come there to Joppa were permitted to stay in the room.

If we have ever walked into the room of a deceased where wailing and crying is present we know how distracting this can be. An atmosphere of faith is certainly not created when such emotions pervade a room. The heightened presence of such emotions can easily create a pervasive and overriding atmosphere of unbelief. Imagine trying to minister in this atmosphere. If Jesus could do no mighty works because of overriding unbelief, then it stands to reason that we will not be able to either.

Peter knew what needed to be done when he arrived at the place where Dorcas lay. He had already experienced a similar scenario. He accompanied Jesus to the ruler's house where the unruly unbelievers were put outside. Peter knew that the best way to mobilize the atmosphere and environment was by ridding the emotional individuals from the room. All the unbelief needed to go so faith could come forth.

Peter, unlike Jesus, went into the room alone to minister to Dorcas. Jesus, however, permitted certain individuals to enter in with him. Luke 8:51 lets us know Jesus permitted the mother and father of the daughter, and Peter, James and John to come into the room with Him. He allowed these five individuals to eye-witness the resurrection of the little girl.

The atmosphere and environment of unbelief in both these instances were well within the reach of Jesus and Peter to control.

For many reasons, it may not always be possible to control the unbelief. It could depend on the point in time when outside believers come on the scene and enter into the picture. It could be later on in a funeral procession.

MINISTERING IN FRONT OF OTHERS WHEN EXPECTED

The most well-known biblical story of a deceased being raised from the dead in front of others involves the story of Lazarus (John 11). You have undoubtedly heard this story repeated countless times if you have been in Christian circles for any length of time. Just because you may have repeatedly heard this story over and over again does not mean that you can not perceive the value of it from another perspective.

Let's take a look at this story from the perspective of who was present when Jesus commanded Lazarus to come forth. Jesus came on the scene and asked Martha and Mary where they had laid Lazarus. They responded by telling Him in verse 34 to *"come and see"*.

Jesus knew what was going to take place when He arrived at Lazarus' grave. Martha and Mary could not comprehend this fact even though Jesus had stated that Lazarus would rise again. They perceived Him to be talking about the end-time resurrection.

Jesus could have pulled Martha and Mary aside to tell them to just sit tight until all the people left. When they said *"come and see"* He could have told them that He wanted just the three of them to go to Lazarus' grave alone. He did not. To perhaps understand why Jesus was not concerned about other people going to the grave site, we should really try to grasp the picture of what was stirring within Him at this point.

Verse 33 states that Jesus *"groaned in the spirit, and was troubled"*, especially after He saw Mary and the other Jews with her that were weeping. The word "groan" in the Greek means to "snort with anger; to have indignation; to sternly enjoin" (Strongs Greek Hebrew

Concordance #1690). Jesus was like an angry, pawing bull that was snorting with a righteous anger and indignation at what had happened to Lazarus. Jesus was *"troubled"*. He was so troubled and angry that the next verse 35 tells us, *"Jesus wept."*

The emotion behind the manifestation of Jesus' crying was that of anger and indignation, not to mention the possibility of other looming issues that He knew He was about to face at the cross — mainly His own death. It stands to reason that there was no way Jesus was about to sit still and smile until all the people cleared out. He was ready to approach the spirit of death without delay and hesitation.

Ridding all the individuals who had gathered around to grieve by asking them to leave was not a consideration. His preoccupation with who was around or what they saw was secondary. John 11:19 states that, *"... many of the Jews had joined the women around Martha and Mary, to comfort them concerning* [the death of] *their brother."* We see that there were *"many"* Jews around.

Verse 37 tells us that on the way to Lazarus' grave some of these people said within earshot of Jesus, *"Could not this Man, who opened the eyes of the blind, also have kept this man from dying?"* Verse 38 tells us that Jesus groaned once again. The comments of these people did not interfere or delay the intentions of Jesus while en route to Lazarus' grave. If anything, their statements of unbelief stirred Him up to go after the spirit of death even more because He groaned one more time.

Jesus said the following words to the Father with regard to these individuals who were accompanying Him to Lazarus' grave. He said, that *"they may believe that You sent Me."* Jesus still managed to keep the heart of the people central even though He was troubled. He wanted this particular crowd of people to know He was sent from God so they would give God glory and believe in Him.

Jesus then placed Himself in a fixed position and became the intermediary between death and Lazarus in front of all these individuals. We know that He, being in a righteously indignant state of mind, *"cried with a loud voice"* and said, *"Lazarus, come forth".* Glory to God...! Can you imagine the intensity of how His next words may have sounded – *"Loose him, and let him go"* – as the individuals became awestruck.

The purpose for addressing death in front of these people proved fruitful. We know that many, not all, of these individuals ended up believing on Him (John 11:45-46). The situation ended up being what Jesus desired for the most part. Lazarus was raised, and many believed.

Let this story be another lesson of insight and wisdom. We may not always sense the need to control for the other individuals present, particularly if they do not appear to pose a threat and interfere with what is taking place. Therefore, we should remain open for mobilizing ourselves to raise the dead in front of others with this same purpose in mind. God may want to show Himself strong to others by allowing them to see and experience a resurrection as well.

On the other hand, there may not be anything that we can do about the presence of other believers.

PRAYING IN THE PRESENCE OF OTHERS WHEN NOT REQUESTED

Have you ever wondered what it will be like for Christians to just spontaneously step forward in front of others without a moment's notice and demonstrate the resurrection power of God? I have. In short, this day is coming to willing Christians. It will certainly take an unconventional act of faith to step forward but it will begin to happen in the earth.

One of the most impressive biblical stories along this line involves the son of the widow at Nain. We can once again extract another valuable insight from this story. We can look at it from the perspective of a believer stepping out with actions of faith that are totally unsolicited. Not only are the actions totally unsolicited, but they are in front of unsuspecting unbelievers and believers.

One of the most poignant points of this story is that it prophetically represents the anticipated level of maturity within the Body of Christ in overcoming the earthly enemy of death. It is an open showdown where the supernatural power of the Holy Spirit easily dispels and discredits the power of death through the faith-filled actions of Jesus.

An injustice would be done in emphasizing the presence of others if the stage was not properly set for this story that is found in Luke 7:11-16.

Jesus was going about His Father's business one day when He ended up coming upon the middle of a funeral procession. It was the funeral for the only son of a widow. Jesus did not have a personal relationship with this woman or her son in the natural sense of the word; nor did He have a relationship with anyone connected to this woman that we know of. What we do know is that Jesus was not approached and requested to step forward to minister to the deceased.

Jesus knew in His spirit, like we will come to know in ours, that He was in the right place at the right time as the events about to unfold on His part were completely spontaneous and unsolicited.

> [11]*"Now it happened, the day after, that He went into a city called Nain; and many of His disciples went with Him, and a large crowd.*
> [12]*And when He came near the gate of the city, behold, a dead man was being carried out, the only son of his mother; and she was a widow. And a large crowd from the city was with her.*
> [13]*When the Lord saw her, He had compassion on her and said to her, "Do not weep."*

¹⁴Then He came and touched the open coffin, and those who carried him stood still. And He said, "young man, I say to you, arise."

¹⁵So he who was dead sat up and began to speak. And He presented him to his mother.

¹⁶Then fear came upon all, and they glorified God, saying, "A great prophet has risen up among us"; and, "God has visited His people."

Luke 7:11-16

We should really zero in on the big picture here to realize the impact of the moment. There was a large crowd following Jesus, and, there was a large crowd from the city with the widow. There was the unbelieving and the believing who suddenly found themselves standing opposite each other as Jesus stepped forward. It was a set-up for an open show of the overcoming power of God.

As the old saying goes, you probably could have heard a pin drop as Jesus spontaneously stepped forward. The eyes of all the people became fixed on Him as the carriers of the coffin suddenly stood still when Jesus stepped forward. After all, He was actually interrupting a funeral procession.

Who, in their right mind, would consider doing such an unthinkable and unconventional thing in front of all these people?! Nobody in *their* "right mind" and conventional way of thinking would do this. A faith-filled Christian who possessed the mind of Christ about raising the dead and a sensing of the Holy Spirit would step forward to do this.

Evidently, Jesus was not concerned about what anyone in the crowd would think when He stepped forward and commanded the son to *"Arise"*. Jesus knew what His heavenly Father was thinking. He knew that God was open for this son's life to be restored to his body if He stepped forward at this opportune moment. And so it was, that life was restored to the deceased in his coffin.

For all we know, some of the people in the crowd might have scattered rather quickly when they saw the widow's son sit up and begin talking. Who knows? What we do know is that believers in this day and time will have to remain open and expect that the same thing could possibly happen to us one day. It may not necessarily be in this same type of setting, but there may be many other people around.

We would not want to miss the small window of opportunity to capture the moment and step forward just because other people may be standing by on the scene.

A PERIPHERAL ISSUE

Works of faith to raise the dead in front of others will require some wisdom and spiritual discernment. Whether we choose to minister to a deceased alone, or in front of others, will be a matter of spiritual maturity. The presence of others will gradually begin to become a peripheral consideration and not an imminent one as we continue to gain more experience, wisdom and insight into this dimension.

The faith of cutting edge Christians to unabashedly minister to a deceased in front of others is sure to become a working reality within the Body of Christ. We cannot stop here though. These actions will only take us to the point of ministering life to the deceased. Now we will need to concern ourselves with the issue of how long to stay in the situation and minister before the deceased is raised.

CHAPTER ELEVEN

~

COMMAND AND STAND

"I shall not die, but live, and declare the works of the Lord."

Psalms 118:17

Has it dawned on you that stories in the New Testament pertaining to deceased individuals being raised reveal that all of them were raised immediately? An exception to this is provided in the Old Testament. The individual ministering to the deceased had to persist in order to prevail. Otherwise, immediate results were always obtained.

Perhaps many of us have found ourselves ministering in a death situation only to be let down because the deceased was not immediately raised. After all, this is our perception of how it should happen. Right? This is how the results came about for Jesus. However, Jesus still had to develop and mature into His earthly ministry to attain these results even though He was a perfect man. We should expect to follow this pattern in order to develop as well.

"Develop" is the key word to hone in on. Arriving at a place of maturity is an ongoing and developing process. Maturity does not occur overnight no matter what field or occupation wherein we find ourselves. Our respective occupation can still be difficult at times when we do reach a heightened level of maturity. The dimension of believers raising the dead can be likened to this same process.

Accordingly, the Body of Christ has some developing to do when it comes to raising the dead. This may require some further actions of faith to be taken past the immediate stage of ministry to a deceased.

THE EXPERIENCE OF OTHERS

The author has made a conscious and deliberate effort thus far to adhere strictly to the Bible and the documentary video, *Raised From The Dead*, as reference sources. This measure has been taken primarily for the sake of validity and credibility. A deviation from these two references will begin to factor into the picture at this point, and for good reason.

Since we find no stories in the Bible where individuals unsuccessfully attempted to raise the dead, believers have no other choice but to look elsewhere for some insight and wisdom on this matter. We are left to discreetly study the successful experiences of other believers, aside from the Bible, who have raised the dead in the Name of Jesus Christ. We can then observe how long it took for deceased individuals to be raised.

As we will see, believers may have to patiently endure a maturing process by learning to stand the test of time when ministering to a deceased. For this reason, we should not be too quick to put on the brakes in these situations if the deceased is not immediately raised. Time may have to become our friend.

TIME WILL TELL

The first time we begin to minister to a deceased can be likened to a doctor performing his first surgery. The surgery may take a little longer to perform due to the lack of skill and experience. Nonetheless, the operation will be completed even though it will take more time than if an experienced surgeon performed the same surgery.

The more the same surgical process is refined with experience, the less time it will take to do the surgery. This refining process is hoped for even though innumerable variables can still interfere and greatly affect the end result. A doctor and his team do not just give up and walk away if unforeseen complications and resulting delays arise. No, they hang in there until they are finished.

Those of us desiring to raise the dead would be wise to keep these same principles in mind. We should approach these situations with the mind-set of committing to them if the desired results are not immediately obtained. We may have to stand the test of that ugly four-letter word called *time* in order to see the desired results come about. This need to commit to these situations for the desired outcome has been borne out by the experience of others.

Let's take a brief look at one biblical story and three modern day stories in order to bring this point home. We will then be able to see how endurance and persistence pays off when initial efforts of ministry are to no avail.

ELISHA

The prophet, Elisha, is a prime and radical example of perseverance and unconventional faith where a resurrection situation is concerned. Just to refresh your memory, the entire passage of Scripture in 2 Kings 4:8-37 is the story about Elisha and his servant, Gehazi. They are the ones who ministered life to the deceased young son of the Shunnamite woman.

Elisha first sent Gehazi to the Shunnamite woman's home to minister to the little boy. Gehazi went upstairs to the room to minister life to the little boy but he was not raised. Elisha arrived on the scene some time later with the boy's mother. He went upstairs to minister to the young child as well.

One of the ways in which Elisha ministered is well stated in verse 34. It states that Elisha, *"...went up and lay on the child, and put his mouth on his mouth, his eyes to his eyes, and his hands on his hands; and then stretched himself out on the child, and the flesh of the child became warm"*, but the little boy did not come back to life.

(It would be very easy to get sidetracked with *how* Elisha ministered to this boy. Please note that I *am not* advocating that we approach a deceased in this fashion. Elisha did what he felt he needed to do, under the Old Testament Covenant, to see life restored to this child. The point of focus here remains on the fact that Elisha did not see immediate results, not *how* he got them. We are under a new covenant established upon better promises.)

Elisha then walked out of the room and paced back and forth in the house for an undisclosed period of time when the child did not come back to life. The Bible does not let us in on any of Elisha's thoughts, but you can only imagine the battle racing through his mind during this time. Even then, he had to continue with further actions if the child was going to be raised. He did not give up when his initial efforts failed. He continued to persevere and press in to the situation.

He went back upstairs a second time. This time he was even more determined to prevail upon the grip that death had on this little boy. Elisha stretched himself out over the child once again. This time the child sneezed seven times and then opened his eyes.

Life was totally restored to this little boy but it did not come without a good fight of faith from Elisha. This story should be an insightful lesson to those who find themselves in situations where the deceased is not immediately raised. There should be no hurry to dismiss the idea of ministering to a deceased to be raised just because they do not immediately respond.

Elisha could not overcome the threshold of death in his initial efforts but he did not quit. We do not know how much time lapsed from the time Elisha initially arrived in the room until the child was raised. We do know that he stayed at that place and continued fighting a good fight of faith until he got the intended results.

NNEKA AND PASTOR DANIEL

If you will remember, in the chapter *A Modern Day Story,* Pastor Daniel did not immediately arise when the believers began ministering to him. They continued the process by singing songs of praise and worship unto the Lord for a while. Even then, Pastor Daniel's body did not respond. When these actions did not work they kept pressing in to the situation.

Those present began to reason among themselves that the stiffness needed to be massaged out of his body. They began massaging Pastor Daniel's arms and turning his neck. His body *finally* began to respond to their ministry.

The point here is that Pastor Daniel did not immediately rise. It took some time. The next modern day story provides us with a more definitive time frame.

PASTOR JONI

This story stems out of the ministry of Heidi and Rolland Baker in Maputo, Mozambique, Africa. The Bakers were ministering to and teaching a group of twelve pastors. Heidi prophesied to two of the pastors, named Rego and Joni, during these meetings. She gave them a prophetic charge to start believing for the dead to be raised.

Both of these pastors returned to their villages with this prophetic word obviously seared in their heart. It wasn't very long before this prophetic word was put to the test for Pastor Joni. Pastor Joni was approached to come minister to a deceased woman in the village soon thereafter who had just died from cholera.

Pastor Joni arrived and began ministering, and ministering, and ministering. Finally, *three hours later,* the woman began to move on her own volition as resurrection life *slowly* began returning to her body[1].

ARJUN

The next story is about a five-year-old boy from New Delhi, India, named Arjun Janki Dass. Arjun died from an accidental electrocution. Medical doctors worked on his body for about two hours, but to no avail. His parents were then told that they needed to call a mortician. They called a minister at a nearby Deliverance Church instead. The minister then called upon one of his staff members to attend to the situation.

This staff member and two other Christians went to Arjun's home to minister, alongside the parents. The five of them began ministering to the dead body at about 10:00 that night. They fervently ministered for *six hours* before Arjun suddenly snapped back to life.

The only evidence of the electrocution today is a nasty scar behind his left ear where the wire hit him.[2]

TIME & METHODS

The author has read many stories where a deceased was raised back to life, and has come to some general conclusions. There are no set time frames for ministering to a deceased. Neither are there any set-in-stone procedures. The ministry time varies as well as the methods of ministering.

---

1. Toronto Airport Christian Fellowship, *Spread The Fire,* Issue 2 — 2003.
2. Rutz, James, *Megashift,* Empowerment Press, Colorado Springs, Colorado, USA, 2005, p. 3.

The time involved for seeing that deceased individuals are resurrected have ranged from immediate results to several hours of constant and persistent ministry. One resurrection even took place, off-and-on, over a three-day period.[3] Obviously, it looks as if ongoing actions of faith is one contributing factor that determines the time frame for ministry.

The method and manner of hands-on ministry within these stories also varied as much as the time element. Some laid the Bible on the deceased. Others read the Word of God over them. Many sang and prayed while others spoke in tongues. Some used a rotating ministry team in order to continue ministering without interruption. And the list goes on.

No matter how long we minister or the methods we use, God will have to be convinced that we are convinced that the deceased will come back to life. Needless to say, our faith will be tested to see if we can be swayed to buy in to the unbelief that the deceased cannot be raised. The test of time is sure to be a major consideration in this regard.

With these things in mind, we would be wise to put on our work clothes when going to minister to a deceased. We should go and expect for immediate results, but be prepared for the duration.

HOW LONG

Only God knows how long it will truly take before a deceased to whom we minister will respond. We can see that it is extremely helpful if a belief system for raising the dead is already established, whether we are a living loved one or a ministering believer. The endurance of grief-stricken, living loved ones to let us exercise our faith for an extended period of time can become a crucial variable. A

---

3. Ibid, p. 104-5.

true story experienced by the author with this issue in mind follows, and is used with the woman's permission.

SUSAN

One morning I received a telephone call from a woman whom I shall refer to as Susan. Susan knew *about* the writing of this book. She was justifiably upset when she called. Her older brother, a music leader at his church, was close to death's door after battling esophageal cancer for two years.

Susan specifically called to ask if I would be willing to accompany her to the hospital to minister to her brother. I agreed to go. After about an hour or so into our visit, her brother began gasping for breath. He died, despite efforts by the hospital personnel to keep him alive. The emotional aftermath exhibited by the family members was understandable upon his passing.

As I stood and watched this man die, I knew within my spirit that his life did not have to be over. He had shared with me on earlier occasion that he wanted to continue living. Susan requested of her sister-in-law that I be allowed to have some time alone to minister to this man. Approximately three hours later, I was allowed to go in the room alone and minister life to this man after family members and friends finished coming in to pay their respects.

I began ministering to this man while his wife was taking care of administrative issues with the hospital. The wife decided that her husband was not going to be raised after I had been ministering to him for about 30-35 minutes. She, her husband's daughter, and Susan entered the room.

Upon entering the room all three of these individuals witnessed and verified this man's body to be *warm*. There was a glimmer of hope to be able to continue ministering for a few seconds, when his warm body temperature was realized, but it did not last long. Understandably, the wife simply endured all she could and the time for ministry ceased. Likewise, other living loved ones may reach a stopping point if the deceased is not immediately raised.

On a similar note, the living loved ones may tell you up front that you only have so much time to minister. Respect their desires and authority when this is the case. Enter into the situation and minister for the time granted. Minister as if it were *your* deceased loved one.

Our goal in each situation should be to commit to it until there is a release. Either the deceased will be raised, we will continue until we are stopped, or we will sense a release to cease ministering. We can readily surmise from these outcomes that time will be a compelling and telling factor.

No matter how much time we have, God will have to be convinced that we are convinced that the deceased will live again.

SPECIFIC EXPECTATIONS

There is another vitally important aspect of ministry to discuss in the way of raising the dead. It pertains to the expectations that we have of a body's condition when it is to be resurrected. In short, Jesus expected deceased individuals to come back whole, and not with the sickness that killed them. We should minister with this same intent.

This is not to say that if the deceased does not come back healed that we should get under condemnation. Realistically speaking, some resurrections may not reflect our specific expectations. Knowing this, we should do what we know to do for the sake of covering the basis, and keep our expectations in check.

With this in mind, what I am about to say is very important. We should be very specific to God about what we expect in the way of a body's condition upon being raised, when we minister to a deceased. Our stated desire should be for the body to be restored and made whole. This fact can become especially important when trying to ignore the shocking condition of a body lying before us.

The author is well aware of one credible and verifiable story that best brings this point home, but the identity will remain anonymous for the sake of wisdom and discretion. This is one of many stories to come that can be used to advance the educational aspects of this dimension. In retrospect, this situation should be utilized for educational purposes in looking forward.

BE MADE WHOLE

An individual died as a result of a head-on car collision with a tractor trailer truck. This person was immediately ushered into heaven whereupon he was greeted by people he had known during his life on earth. Back on earth, virtually every bone in this victim's body had been broken or shattered. Two of his limbs had been completely severed.

Another believer came upon the scene shortly thereafter. This believer asked God for the deceased individual to live. Specifically, the believer also requested that there be no "head injuries" or "internal injuries". Miraculously, the spirit of the deceased returned to the body, and there were no head injuries or internal injuries. But, there were a lot broken bones to overcome, and a long and painful road of rehabilitation ahead.

Thank God this individual lived, and that the believer who came upon the scene had the spiritual maturity to exercise his faith for life to be restored to the deceased. However, we can learn from this situation one of the many invaluable lessons to come. We should be specific to God up front about how we expect the end result to be in way of the spirit, soul and body when a deceased is raised. We will get what we ask for from God. With this in mind, we need to be increasingly aware of what we are specifically asking in these situations.

We will have to learn to ignore what we see in the natural and specifically address what we expect to take place in the way of the spiritual. Ask that the deceased be made whole to arise and walk in newness of life when they are resurrected. It is one issue to have life restored. It is another issue altogether to be made whole.

FEET OFF THE BRAKES

It is obvious that we may have to take our feet off the brakes and enter into some uncharted territory if immediate results are not obtained in these situations. The road to a resurrection may take longer than we think. Believers will have to think about crossing even more conventional thresholds in order to get down this road when it comes to the time factor.

For instance, take the situation of Jesus when He ministered to Lazarus and apply it to us today. Jesus walked up to the grave site and commanded others to remove the stone so Lazarus would be able to come forth out of the grave where he was laid. Likewise, someone may have to step forward and open a casket at the end of a funeral so a deceased can rise when they are being ministered to.

Learning to stand the test of time and taking further actions of faith in these situations could very well be what determines the beginning of our success. Regardless of the outcome, our experiences in this regard can only serve to bring greater maturity for future situations down the road. Hopefully, our future situations will render immediate results on a more consistent basis as we learn to command life to come, and stand on the Word of God while believing for a deceased to live and be made whole.

Having provided the reader with the referenced stories and morsels of insight and wisdom, the answer to the question of how long we should minister to a deceased merits one simple answer — as long as it takes.

COME FORTH

The previous two chapters and this one brought home the realization that 1) Christians can intervene at any time; 2) others may or may not be present, and, 3) that we should be prepared to commit to a resurrection situation for the duration. We can see that the limitations are boundless and that the actions of faith are ours for the taking.

We should now have a better feel for how to come forth against the enemy of death, and come forth better equipped than ever before. It may take time to see this dimension corporately manifest within the Body of Christ, but we will see this happen. It goes without saying that, we have our work cut out for us in facing the realities that accompany this dimension.

PART THREE:

PREPARING FOR WORK

This Section will reveal some of the realistic and opposing issues that believers can expect to encounter in raising the dead. The opposition we will face is brought into perspective upon seeing the impact and rippling effects that earthly resurrections will begin to have on the Church. The group of individuals who have no choice but to spearhead this dimension will come into focus as well in this next section.

My objective is to reveal how the earthly Church will need to make this enemy called death the footstool of Jesus Christ before He can be released from the Throne of God.

~

CHAPTER TWELVE

REALITY CHECK

"Have the gates of death been revealed to you? Or have you seen the doors of the shadow of death?"
Job 38:17

You know you are on the right track if the phrase, *"easier said than done"* has already crossed your lips when it comes to raising the dead. Certainly, the author's intent thus far has been to incite the faith of God within you to see the dead raised. While this text has admittedly been subjective in nature, it is only befitting to bring other relevant issues to the table not so subjective, but yet realistic.

A melting pot of complex issues and questions will begin to arise as we make headway into these situations. The nebulous nature of our human faith can readily undermine our confidence to step out in this dimension if not careful. It is for this reason that a few various and sundry issues generally associated with this dimension will be addressed in this chapter. These issues will vary from one end of the spectrum to the other.

Addressing the realistic apprehensions and anxieties upon a decision to initially enter into this dimension is a wise place to first start this discussion. The middle of the chapter will find us addressing the realities of bringing closure to these situations, not to mention dealing with a corpse when it is anything but presentable. We will conclude at the other end of the spectrum by discussing the issue of counterfeit resurrections and how to recognize them.

These issues should serve as a springboard in which to further prepare us for some of the unsuspecting and harsh realities associated with this dimension.

THE "WHAT IF" QUESTION

This author perceives that one of the biggest and subconscious barriers to initially entering into this dimension deals with the big *what if* question. What if we minister to a deceased and they are not raised? Let's face this fact and meet it head on now. There are those individuals who will be resurrected and there will be those that will not.

Many of us may be reluctant to enter into this dimension due to the possibility looming over our heads that a deceased may not be raised. This is one unavoidable possibility that we, as human beings, will have to accept. Remember, we want God's will to be done where the outcome is concerned. Sometimes deceased individuals will be raised and sometimes they will not, and this is the nature of earthly resurrection ministry.

We would be wise to remember that our efforts are relative regardless of the outcome. Relatively speaking, these efforts should also be understood in the corporate sense of the word when someone is not raised. The Church will continue to come up short in seeing the dead raised if the Body of Christ chooses to play it safe by doing nothing when individuals die a premature death. The enemy of death will never be overcome.

Sooner or later we will be challenged to step out in this regard. Will we rise to the occasion? The first time will probably be the most difficult due to lack of experience in this dimension. But remember, God is not looking for experience as much as He needs to see faith; although there is something to be said for experience. Experience will render even more wisdom and insight into these situations. Experience will come but the only way it will come is by doing.

We should much rather assume the risk of exercising actions of faith rather than continuing to do nothing when someone dies a premature death. Only God truly knows what our efforts will render and what is best for everyone involved in these situations.

THE TENDENCY TO DISMISS

Just in case the tendency to dismiss the thought of ministering to deceased individuals still tries to pervade your thinking, think again. Let us reflect upon this *what if* question from a different perspective. Let's think about this issue from the angle of our present ministry abilities.

Have you ever prayed for someone to be healed from sickness? Have you ever prayed for someone to be delivered from demonic influence? The answer to these questions is hopefully, yes. Was everyone that you prayed for healed or delivered in your presence? The answer to this question is probably, no. Did you stop to ask, "What if they are not healed or delivered?", before you prayed for them? You probably did not.

You probably continued ministering, and still continue to minister in this same capacity, even though individuals were not healed or delivered when you ministered. Does this mean that you are a failure? No. Does this mean you should back off and not minister any more? Absolutely not. You should continue on with your ministry because you still believe in healing and deliverance. And so it is with raising the dead. Truth is still truth whether it can be demonstrated or not. It just makes it more acceptable when it can be.

We should not use our shortcomings as an excuse to absolve ourselves from ministering in this capacity. If anything, they should be used as an experience that will make us even more determined to overcome death. They should serve to push us forward, and not allow them to cause us to draw back the next time death crosses our path.

Raising the dead will be a time of challenge for the Body of Christ to begin taking different actions of faith. Take note: It will take a paradigm shift in our thinking in order to start entering into this dimension. Our thinking and actions will progressively begin to transition and shift away from a *what if they do not rise* mode the more we establish the Word of God in our spirit and acquire understanding of this dimension.

When a true shift in our thinking begins to settle into place, an active and offensive posture will be assumed instead of a passive and hesitant one.

ACKNOWLEDGING OUR HUMANITY

A realistic issue associated with this *what if* question merits genuine concern. *What if* a deceased is not raised when we minister to them? The grim results are readily visible and staring us in the face when this is the outcome. What would we do then? This is a realistic issue that consequently should be addressed.

Deeply rooted in the *what if* mentality is the reality of having to face living loved ones and other individuals when a deceased is not raised. In other words, the results cannot be escaped by the believers doing the ministering when someone is not raised. Raising the dead is not a *move on down the prayer line* type of ministry.

Believers will have to humbly bring the time of ministry to a close when it looks as if a deceased is not going to be raised. There will be heartbroken and grieving loved ones for us to face who will never see their deceased loved one on this earth again. The prospect of having to face these heartbreaking situations can be an humbling experience to say the least. We will have no other choice but to stop and face the reality of our human limitations in an humbling manner.

Efforts should then be made to comfort the living loved ones during their time of grief. There still is a redeeming factor in the midst of the situation even when the results are not what we earnestly hoped. Living loved ones can take solace in the fact that they did everything humanly AND spiritually possible in order to see that the deceased was raised.

GOING BACK

We all have deceased loved ones we would dearly love to see again. The outcome of their lives could possibly have been different if the revelation of this text had been secured under our belts long before things went prematurely awry. Arrangements for them might have been handled quite differently. Nevertheless, a lack of knowledge on this subject, a lack of willing individuals, and a lack of faith to carry out actions of faith were missing at the time.

We will continually have to learn how to wisely appropriate the truths of this dimension now that this revelation is being illuminated to our understanding. Having said this, it has been the author's experience that one common thread tends to consistently resurface by grieving individuals longing to see their deceased loved ones again. It is the issue of wanting to *go back* and minister life to their deceased loved one who has been dead for an extended period of time after the burial.

Going back is relative to the time frame to which one may be alluding. The length of the time frame is what we should hone in on.

How far to *go back* becomes the crux of this issue. From the outset, we should avoid putting God in a box by saying how far we can go back. God can override our human limitations and go far beyond what we could ever think or ask of Him when faith for such is present.

First we should look to the Scriptures for any instance where someone went back to minister to a deceased. The one instance this author found was where Jesus deliberately went back to a burial site for the specific purpose of seeing someone raised. He went to the grave of Lazarus after Lazarus had already been buried.

The time frame within which these actions took place was *shortly after* Lazarus was buried. We know this to be true because friends were still gathered at Martha and Mary's house when Jesus arrived. Jesus did not *go back* after an extended period of time from the time of the death. Of course, there is no succinct definition of *extended period* either.

The definition of *extended period* and *shortly thereafter* will have to come from the Spirit of the Lord to those who have the faith to believe God to *go back* to a burial site. The phrase that comes to mind pertains to Ezekial 37, "can these bones live again?" So be it according to the actions of faith willing to be taken by these believing individuals. On the other hand, perhaps the underlying need of someone wanting to *go back* is the need for some closure while walking out the grieving process.

Everyone has deceased loved ones they dearly long to see again. This desire is especially aroused even more when the revelation of how to go about raising the dead is acquired. The harsh reality of this arousal is that a deceased loved one who has been gone for an *extended period* of time will probably not be seen again in this life unless it is *shortly thereafter*. We can only go back so far given our human limitations.

On this point, we should remember that God is one day going to make it right in the end for those who choose to believe on the

Lord Jesus Christ as the one and only Son of the living God.

SEEING AND TOUCHING DEATH

We would be wise to keep in the back of our mind that we cannot always assume a corpse will be pleasant to look upon. This ugliness is further compounded when the condition of the corpse is anything but presentable. If we can envision praying for a deceased whose body may be swollen, distended, skeletal, emaciated, diseased, decomposing, then we can see a realistic picture. The trail of death is not always a pretty picture.

> *The trail of death is not always a pretty picture.*

Some individuals are used to being around these kinds of lifeless bodies, especially in third world countries. Individuals in many of these places are used to handling their own deceased loved ones. The western world is quite different. The thought of touching or smelling bodies in these conditions for the purpose of ministering to them could be difficult for many Westerners. Then again, who says that we have to touch a deceased in order to minister to them?

The case of Lazarus provides a classic illustration of this point. Jesus never touched Lazarus. He addressed his body and spirit from a distance. He probably had no intentions of going in the burial tomb after four days of death.

Like Jesus, we can exercise our faith at a distance and for good reason when unpleasant circumstances abound. The possibility very well exists that we may someday find ourselves called upon to enter into conditions of this sort. Every experience will be unique, and to be forearmed as much as possible will help.

Recreating, refashioning or reshaping a vile-looking corpse is easy for God to do. In order to bring perspective to this fact, remember that countless millions of bodies without flesh are going to be restored and resurrected in the end time. Restoring one body is minuscule compared to what is going to take place.

The real issue in these types of gruesome situations is whether or not we can take the necessary actions of faith in order to see life-giving flesh regenerate upon a body. The choices will be ours according to our faith and how we choose to address the situation, sometimes even in the ugliest face of death.

The famous actor, Clint Eastwood, used a quote that seems most befitting in this regard. "A man's gotta know his limitations." It is the author's opinion that we may have just discovered the beginning of ours — when death appears too ugly for us to humanly confront.

COUNTERFEIT RESURRECTIONS

We have briefly covered an array of issues pertaining to some of the realities that can be expected when encountering this dimension. Now let's go to the deep end of the spectrum where one reality stands out on its own. It is the reality of a counterfeit to this move of God. It is that of counterfeit resurrections.

Counterfeiting is solely predicated upon deception. The devil goes to great lengths to devise deceptive schemes in order to counterfeit what God is doing in the earth today. For this reason, we need to be able to recognize counterfeit situations for what they are when they occur.

We would be wise to keep in mind that there are two distinct and different types of resurrections: true and counterfeit. True resurrections are those that happen through the work of the Holy Spirit and in the name of Jesus. Counterfeit resurrections are those that occur aside from the work of God's Holy Spirit and His Son Jesus.

Counterfeits contain just enough elements of the real to deceive us into thinking we are encountering the genuine. The ulterior purpose of a counterfeit is to deceptively inhibit other individuals from being able to recognize, need and desire the real. Satan and his cohorts know how to work through individuals in order to deceive people with regard to whatever it is that God is restoring and doing in the earth.

Raising the dead is no exception to this deception. For this reason, we should not be deceived or caught off guard in thinking that the devil is not attempting to counterfeit this move of the Spirit of God. Just ask those who live in places where voodoo, witchcraft, sorcery and all other kinds of satanic practices are exercised in this manner. It is very real.

People given to satanic practices (and there are plenty of them out there) have learned how to invoke evil power like Christians have learned how to draw upon the power from the Holy Spirit. The following excerpt provides excellent insight into these people and how to recognize counterfeit resurrections for what they are.

> An account of one such diabolical "raising the dead" was given by Frederick Kaigh, an English physician who witnessed it, in Witchcraft and Magic of Africa; it was summarized by Edward Connor in Prophecy for Today (page 129) under the heading: "Can the Devil Raise the Dead?" In this account, an African chief was raised (in order to name his murderer), apparently through the words and actions of a witch doctor. The raising took place at night, and it involved strange preternatural phenomena; at the end of the ceremony the chief walked off down a lane in the moonlight and was seen no more. The accused murderer was found dead the next day, with no explainable reason.

Edward Connor comments: "Despite the impressiveness of the occurrence, it will be apparent that the chief was not returned to life in the sense that Christ gave life back to Lazarus or the widow's son. In true restorations, the person raised from the dead continues a normal life among men. In false restorations, there is no evidence that the soul has been restored to the corpse in anything like its true natural relationship, nor even any evidence that the spirit using the corpse is the soul which originally animated it." [1]

One thing is abundantly clear here. The African chief certainly did not come back with the purpose of giving glory to God through Jesus Christ. He had intentions to murder someone. To address the issue of whether the devil can counterfeit this move by raising the dead is well stated in this article. To the temporary degree that the devil *directly* thwarts God's plans and purposes for earthly resurrections through such a diabolical manner remains to be seen.

A strategic and concerted effort has already been *directly* unleashed by the devil in one regard, in case we have not noticed. This effort plays on the vernacular and semantics of biblical words. In other words, the definition of certain words are played upon by using them in another manner to which we are not accustomed. This manner plays upon the double meaning of the words that Christians would normally use. One only has to take note of the airwaves to observe this fact. After all, the devil is referred to as the "prince of the air" (Ephesians 2:2).

---

1. Father Albert J. Hebert, *Raised From The Dead,* Tan Books and Publishers, Inc.,

For instance, have you noticed that the words "supernatural", "miracles" and "resurrection" have all been used by the media as the name of certain television shows? If the advertisements truly reflect the content of these shows, they are not in keeping with what Christians deem a God-ordained supernatural happening, miracle or resurrection. Those who are spiritually discerning can readily pinpoint this strategy, but those with carnal eyes can only digest it in the diabolical and perverted way in which it is presented to them.

This strategy is no coincidence. Down the road, many of these same individuals would have the tendency to dismiss the reality and possibility of the miracle working, supernatural and resurrection power of God when it crossed their path. This is because the possibility now exists that they would associate these words with being scary and spooky. In other words, they are unable to properly discriminate between good and evil.

This perspective may sound absurd to some, but not to discerning believers in Jesus Christ who know better. Nevertheless, it is a very subtle and calculated strategy by the devil. Its design is intended to condition the minds of individuals to attach an undermining definition and questionable nature to acts associated with these words. This is especially true when it comes to earthly resurrections.

If individuals' minds can be conditioned to associate raising the dead with spooky and cultish activity, people will automatically shy away from acknowledging true resurrections of the Holy Spirit. They will shy away from God, and the gospel of Jesus Christ, if this type of evil power is associated with Him. This response is exactly what the devil wants to elicit from people. It is for reasons such as this that the Bible admonishes us in Hebrews 5:14 that we should have our spiritual senses exercised in order to discern between good and evil.

Along this line, there is one rule of thumb that we should remember, and that will help us to properly discern and discriminate between true and false resurrections in the future. Counterfeit and diabolical resurrections play on the fears of man. They draw attention to another other than Jesus Christ. True resurrections point people toward Jesus Christ.

STAY ON COURSE

This chapter has provided only a few of the realistic issues we could expect to encounter in our endeavors. Many others are sure to arise as we venture out into this dimension. The idea behind presenting these realities is that we stay on course and finish the good fight of faith without being sidetracked by the realistic distractions that are sure to come our way.

It becomes increasingly apparent to see why the devil will continue to cast an ongoing atmosphere of suspicion and deception in the earth regarding the idea of Christians raising the dead. As we will begin to see, many people can be influenced to turn to the Lord Jesus Christ when someone is raised.

~

CHAPTER THIRTEEN

...AND MANY BELIEVED

"Go and tell (John) the things which you hear
and see:...the dead are raised up..." Blessed is he
who is not offended because of Me.

Matthew 11:4-7

One Sunday night my son's church youth group and several adults went to the local bowling alley for a night of fun. A particular gentleman and I found ourselves engaged in a pleasant conversation about this subject of Christians raising the dead. Another man had quietly eased himself within earshot of our conversation. He had obviously become offended at what he was hearing and inappropriately ended up in our conversation.

It quickly became apparent that this was going to be one of those unexpected situations where wisdom dictated that I hold my peace. I allowed this same man to continue on. He was, in essence, standing firm in his stance about what raising the dead meant. His opinion was that *raising the dead* should be construed more from a symbolic point of view and not a literal one.

His belief was that *raising the dead* refers to raising the unsaved people in the world who are alive, but yet *dead* in their trespasses and sins. He emphatically stated that these were the individuals with whom we should concern ourselves with resurrecting and not literal dead people. A wise response slowly began to stir within me as I allowed this man to continue talking.

I began to *see* that he really did have a very relevant issue to what I was writing. He deemed his perceptions to be relevant in one regard. I began to perceive them as relevant in another regard. At about this same time, the man brought his stance to a climactic standstill by posing a point blank question; one for which he apparently assumed I would not have a plausible answer. His question was this: "...so why would anyone want to concern themselves with raising the dead when you've got all these people out here in the world who are dead in their sins and not even saved?"

What follows are the thoughts that were rising up out of the recesses of my spirit before I provided him a simple answer.

"AND MANY BELIEVED ON THE LORD"

Let's look at the story of Dorcas once more from the perspective of what transpired among the people after her resurrection took place (Acts 9:36-43). It is the first story that will help reveal some insight to the answer given to my bowling alley friend.

Verse 42 states that after Dorcas was resurrected, *"it became known throughout all Joppa."* Take note that word of the power and demonstration of God in this manner spread throughout this whole particular region. The fact that word spread throughout the region is important, but not as important as the ensuing responses of the people.

The Bible goes on to state, *"and many believed on the Lord"* upon receiving news of this miracle. In other words, *many* began to believe on the Lord throughout this whole particular region. There was not just a few who believed. *Many* believed on the Lord, and Peter ended up staying many days as a result.

Objectively speaking, it is worth noting that while *many* believed, not *all* believed on Him. Some individuals simply cannot fathom or digest the fact that a dead person can be raised. The thought of this happening is far beyond their present ability to spiritually comprehend. They simply will refuse to believe.

Accordingly, we should be cautious in assuming that just because a deceased is resurrected that an unbeliever will automatically want to believe in *someone* that *raises dead people*. We should first try to see what unbelievers see in order to understand how this can happen. We have to go back to the perception that many attach to the idea of the dead being raised.

Raising the dead, outside the scope of knowing Jesus Christ, is many times often associated by others as satanic or evil. Automatically, people will turn off and dismiss the very idea upon hearing that someone is being raised from the dead. These people really may not want anything to do with raising the dead, much less someone associated with what they perceive is satanic.

Again, we can see why the devil is hard at work to thwart the masses' perceptions about this subject through the air waves. He can keep others from coming to know Jesus Christ if he can keep *raising the dead* as a happening that is associated with evil. This is one prime reason that the focus of these occurrences, when it is not a counterfeit, should remain on Jesus Christ more than the resurrection itself.

Think of all the people you know that do not know, or who refuse to acknowledge Jesus as the Christ, the Son of the living God. They run the risk of not being able to "see" Jesus when someone is raised. In light of this fact, we would be well advised to make sure the name of Jesus is in the same sentence when we talk about raising the dead, especially around unbelievers.

There is no true resurrection aside from Christ Jesus. Selah!

"THE FAME HEREOF WENT ABROAD"
The story of the ruler's daughter being raised by Jesus (in Matthew 9:18-26) yielded a reaction and response from the people similar to when Dorcas was raised. Specifically, Matthew 9:26 in the King James Version provides us with this response: *"...the fame hereof went abroad..."*.

This same story is recorded in Mark 5:35-43. Oddly enough, verse 43 tells us that Jesus gave a strict command *"that no one should know it."* Needless to say, a miracle like this is difficult to contain because, obviously, word leaked out and went abroad.

"THIS REPORT ABOUT HIM WENT THROUGHOUT"
The writer, Luke, discloses a somewhat similar response directed toward Jesus by the individuals who eyewitnessed the resurrection of the widow's son at Nain. (Luke 7:12-17.) Verse 16 states that immediately after the son was raised, *"Then fear came upon all, and they glorified God, saying, 'A great prophet has risen up among us'*; and, *'God has visited His people.'"*

Godly fear came upon *all* of the individuals in this large crowd, not just some. They *all* glorified God upon seeing this resurrection. Notice what took place after the people glorified God. Luke 7:17 further states that, *"...this report about Him went throughout all Judea and the surrounding regions..."*. We would not be presumptuous in saying that this large crowd could not help but talk about what transpired before their very eyes.

Would you talk if you saw a deceased sit up in their coffin during the middle of their own funeral procession? I believe I would. It should then come as no surprise that *all* the *surrounding* geographical *regions* were affected for Jesus after this son was resurrected.

It is the opinion of this author that the Body of Christ can expect earthly resurrections to trigger similar results in a geographic region. Many will come to believe on Jesus as the Christ when word of an earthly resurrection spreads in a given geographical region. The irrefutable power of the Holy Spirit in this manner will once again usher in a heightened awareness of the presence of God in the earth today.

THE RIPPLE EFFECTS

The similar and resulting outcome of these three prior resurrections serve to provide the Body of Christ with further insight. We see what can be expected when Christians begin exercising their God-given rights to raise the dead. Given the day of mass communication in which we live, we can also expect that many will begin to come to believe on Jesus Christ. Whole geographical regions can be affected, be it a city, state or nation.

This response of people coming to the Lord is part of the design of such signs, according to John 20:30-31. These Scriptures reflect one of the times that Jesus appeared to His disciples after he was resurrected. They also inform us that Jesus did many other signs in the presence of His disciples that are not written in the Bible. The stated purpose for the signs that are written in the Bible is **"...that ye might believe that Jesus is the Christ, the Son of God**; *and that believing ye might have life through his name."*

Miracles, signs and wonders will cause the name and fame of Jesus Christ as *the* Son of God to spread even more, especially when Christians start raising the dead. This miracle carries with it the explosive potential, like none other, to compel individuals to turn to Jesus Christ. The ripple effects of these happenings should not be ignored.

Repentance, salvation, church growth, and ministry training, are prime examples of what could begin to transpire as Christians start raising the dead. Leaders within the Body of Christ should naturally prepare to handle these responses as this miracle continues happening on a more frequent basis. Extra church services may need to be held at first in order to accommodate people coming to the house of God. Teaching and training individuals on how to minister salvation and repentance to others might be considered as well.

Overall, the rippling effects of this miracle should not be overlooked and underestimated. These suggestions will make more sense when the practice of Christians raising the dead becomes more integrated and accepted within the Church. The following modern day resurrection stories bear out the fact that the Body of Christ can expect to begin experiencing spiritual renewal, especially in terms of salvation and repentance.

SURPRESA SITHOLE

An African man, by the name of Surpresa Sithole, is the Mozambican national director of Iris Ministries, spearheaded by Heidi and Rolland Baker. In February 2001, Supresa was holding a crusade in the community hall of Komatipoort, a small town on the border of Mozambique. An area chief came and told him that the meetings he was conducting would have to be stopped. A six-year-old girl, named Shansha, had died of malaria the night before in a nearby house and people wanted quiet in the area so they could mourn.

Surpressa responded by going to the house seeking permission to minister to the *family*. The mother and six other ladies were at the house, while the little girls' father was gone trying to find transport to take the little girl to the mortuary. The mother permitted Surpresa to come in and minister. He went in and began praying for the family, including Shansha.

Supresa observed that Shansha's cold, stiff body had begun to smell of decay as he started ministering. Nevertheless, he prayed and lingered at the house for a while as the ladies fell asleep, on grass mats on the cement floor. He kept ministering for another hour, not knowing what else to do. All of a sudden the little girl grabbed Surpresa's fingers and sat up as though she had been in a deep sleep.

Surpresa woke up the mother and the ladies. In shock of seeing the little girl alive, they began weeping, laughing and jumping with joy as they ran screaming the news into the village. As a result, the ministry meetings continued to pack audiences in that village for the next two weeks and "many were saved."[1]

REPENTANCE

Souls will not only be saved from hell as Christians start raising the dead, but the convicting power that brings sinners to repentance and right standing before God will manifest as well. Again, this fact is once again borne out in our previous resurrection story of Pastor Daniel and Nneka right after he was raised, and, which is provided in their documentary.

Ministry services were taking place upstairs in the church as dead Pastor Daniel was being ministered to by the church's deliverance ministers. Individuals attending the services upstairs were informed in the meantime about what was transpiring with Pastor Daniel downstairs. Pastor Daniel was consequently ushered upstairs after he had been raised so all of the people could see what God had done. Needless to say, the awesome presence of God filled the auditorium. The Spirit of the Lord began to brood over the entire place as faith began to rise within the place.

A lame woman rose up and threw her crutches aside when she saw Pastor Daniel. This woman started running, not walking, after she threw her crutches aside! She went running to embrace her

---

1. Toronto Airport Christian Fellowship, *Spread The Fire*, Issue 2—2003, p. 13.

husband but her husband said, "Don't touch me. I am a sinner. I have been committing sin. If you touch me, you may become crippled again." Consequently, he ran to the altar, raised his hands, and started crying. He asked God to forgive all his sins right there at the altar that day.[2]

Just like the Scripture says in Luke 7:16 when the widow at Nain's son was raised, *"then fear came upon all."* This particular man experienced the kind of godly fear that brings about conviction in a person's life. As a result, this man and his wife both received what they needed from God by the mere presence of a man who had been raised from the dead. She received healing in her body. He received repentance in his soul. The door was open to both of them for marital reconciliation.

This author would be surprised if many other miracles did not manifest among the crowd of people that day, including many decisions for salvation unto Jesus Christ.

FOOD FOR THOUGHT

The stories of this chapter certainly provide us with ample food for thought. The fact remains that *many individuals* came and believed in Jesus when someone was raised from the dead, and His name and fame spread into geographical regions when individuals were raised from the dead. In light of the response of the given story in this chapter, a harvest of souls coming to know Jesus Christ is a real probability.

Regardless of any conjectures we can make about a harvest of souls, one fact remains. Many individuals are going to turn and come to Jesus as the Christ when Christians begin raising the dead through

---

2. Christ For All Nations; Reinhard Bonnke, *Raised From The Dead.* Documentary Video (Orlando, FL: Full Flame, LLC) February 2002.

the power of the Holy Spirit. The Body of Christ will need to be prepared to seize the moment and capitalize on the window of ministry opportunities as this move of God continues to unfold and escalate.

It is this author's hope that the *message* of this book will be a resource for your equipping.

THE QUESTION

Now let's go back to the question curtly posed to me by my bowling alley acquaintance. "...so why would anyone want to concern themselves with raising the dead when you've got all these people out here in the world who are dead in their sins and not even saved? The answer provided to him was simply stated. "Because when someone is raised from the dead it can make a believer out of them!"

One only has to look through the eyes of the Early Church to comprehend this fact. No doubt, multitudes, geographical regions, and ultimately nations, will be affected for Jesus. Many will be compelled to believe on Jesus as the Christ, the Son of the living God. Will the Body of Christ be prepared to receive them?

CHAPTER FOURTEEN

~

SPREADING "THE MESSAGE"

> "The harvest truly is great, but the labourers are
> few: Pray ye therefore the Lord of the harvest,
> that He would send forth labourers into his
> harvest."
>
> Luke 10:2

It is going to take an unprecedented mind-set shift within the Body of Christ to assimilate, act upon, and impart this message. Having said that, not everyone we come into contact with will be spiritually ready to receive the revelation of this message. Imparting its truths will certainly require believers to exercise the utmost wisdom in order to enhance and more effectively facilitate its widespread acceptance.

A primary avenue for this message to come about in a wise manner is within structured and educational settings. One of the reasons the Body of Christ has been relatively ineffective in this area is due to a lack of education on this subject. Raising the dead is like any other subject requiring faith. The success of its acceptance will come by hearing what the word of God has to say about this subject. We can better hear about this subject when educational platforms become established for such.

Educational settings can greatly help improve our effectiveness as the Word of God is allowed to be expressed on this subject. Let's go ahead and think through a few suggestions in order to help gain a foothold in this dimension.

DESPISE NOT SMALL BEGINNINGS

Small settings can well serve the purpose of an ideal platform for the growth and maturity of this message. Bible studies, seminars, dialogue sessions, leadership meetings are good examples of viable avenues for initially releasing basic truths pertaining to Christians raising the dead. Many of the larger spiritual groups, such as those of faith, inner healing, deliverance from demonic influence, intercessory prayer, prophetic, healing groups, etc., all emerged within the Body of Christ because someone first brought individuals together to teach them in a small setting.

Each group continues to thrive within the Body of Christ today even though the truths of each of these particular groups were initially met with their fair share of resistance. Training centers exist all over the world today that represents each of these groups. These centers exist because revelation, experience, insight, and wisdom on these subjects were first taught in a small setting, and continue to be taught. This pattern of growth and maturity will be no exception as Christians learn how to give themselves to the dimension of raising the dead.

Leaders will gather people together in small groups. They will begin imparting truths. Interested people will begin to listen and these people will begin to spread the word. Informed individuals will be challenged to act upon their faith based upon the Word of God in order to see a deceased raised. These individuals will share what they have learned from the situation in order to further build upon their faith for the next encounter they experience. And so goes the cycle.

The time has come for the message of believers raising the dead to begin going through this cyclical process as well. It will become as common to talk about raising the dead like we do souls being saved, or the sick being healed. With this in mind, interested ministers, ministry leaders, educational facilitators should give some forethought and consideration to how they can best release this message within their various organizations.

CHRISTIAN ORGANIZATIONS

Denominations, networks, Bible colleges and ministry training centers have been effective avenues for communicating various and sundry truths of God for years. Christians raising the dead is another present truth that should be trumpeted through these same channels today. A beckoning call will continue to resound for educational platforms to be established with this message in mind.

Regardless of the reaction and response that Christian organizations have upon receiving the truths of this message, it is inevitable that their leaders will be confronted with this issue. Their constituents will, sooner or later, have to address this issue in that premature death affects all of us. Desperate individuals will not just sit back and let their loved ones go to an early grave when they realize there is another option. Hopefully, action will be considered.

Some organizations will merely acquiesce and mentally ascend to this message. The implementation of this message may take time for other organizations to absorb and digest before responding. Other organizations will be very receptive. They will immediately begin discussing ways to implement and release the truths of this message.

Often is the case that ministry training centers and certain Bible colleges affiliate with certain networks or denominational organizations. Educational entities such as these usually reflect the beliefs of the affiliated organization. In other words, what is permissible from headquarters is what is allowed to be taught in the training center or college. Hopefully, this message will be embraced by key individuals to the degree that this message is introduced and implemented into the curriculum of their respective educational centers.

Individuals tend to gravitate to places where the power of God is expected and expressed. Christian leaders who desire for the power of God to manifest in this regard should go ahead and begin to wisely embrace the truth of this message with their venues in mind.

CHURCH FACILITIES

The majority of believers have virtually had little choice of venue when it comes to ministering to deceased individuals. We have felt the need to skirt around funeral home employees, hospital personnel, and the like, in that we have not understood the unconventional aspects of this dimension. In other words, believers have thought that they could only minister one time for hopefully twenty minutes without being seen, and that a deceased would be raised. These days are changing to the contrary.

Believers in the Body of Christ are beginning to realize other ways and means for ministry. Like Jesus, who delayed two days in going to minister to Lazarus, we will not feel the need to be in such a hurry to minister to a deceased at the particular place. (John 11:6.) Other places can be arranged if the present resting place does not allow for ministry. For instance, leaders within the houses of God should consider the use of church facilities for this purpose.

The idea of ministering over deceased individuals in a church may sound far-fetched but the author views this fact from a different perspective. If we can have a funeral service in the church then we should, all the more, be willing and able to have a resurrection service in the Church. Ideally, there would be no better place for a resurrection to happen than in the House of God. Think about this fact for a moment.

Has the Church become so mesmerized in Her line of thinking about death that we would think it preposterous to raise a deceased individual *in the Church?* You decide if this is the case by the way you initially responded to this thought. Yes, we should be willing and able to minister resurrection life to deceased individuals within a church, and conduct ourselves in a wise manner in the process.

Even though this idea may require some getting used to, resurrections taking place in a church to the glory of God should become a viable option. They could become an option within our church sooner than we think. We never know when our faith as a leader will be tested. It would help to be somewhat prepared naturally should a deceased be brought to our facility by a grieving loved one.

For example, consider a place in your building where deceased individuals could be brought in for ministry. Careful forethought to designate a room where deceased individuals could be ministered to would be wise if involved in a church building program. This should be a place where:

1. Caskets could discreetly be rolled in where babes in Christ and/or children would not be overwhelmed;
2. A room large enough for intercessors as well as ministers;
3. Worship/praise music could be utilized;
4. Ventilation and access to water are considered.

These are just a few suggestions.

One other suggestion is the use of videos, cameras, and the like. We have already seen from Nneka and Pastor Daniel's story how educationally invaluable these visual aids can be. A word of caution, however, should be heeded regarding the use of such. We would not want to utilize these aids at the expense of grieving family members. Consent and rights to use these type aids should first be obtained from living loved ones beforehand as an ethical consideration.

As a very important note here, the author is extremely mindful of the fact that these suggestions come with a very western and industrialized mind-set. They are useful within an ideal environment when a body is presented to us in an ideal fashion. These conditions will not always be realistic to attain to, especially in third world countries. Essentially, we will have to work in the conditions wherein we find ourselves. They may not be the most preferable, nor to our liking.

Those who reside in third world countries (where many raisings are known to have taken place) may not even have a church building in which to minister resurrection life. They may just have a hot, sweaty, one room mud and stick hut. Other times all they have is each other and faith. After all, it only takes faith for the dead to be raised wherever it may happen

When the idea becomes established within the minds of believers that the Church should accommodate ministry for deceased individuals, Christians will not feel such a sense of urgency any longer to skirt around existing secular and sacred places looking for an open window to minister life. The idea here is that the Body of Christ takes strides and makes advancements that help remove the barriers and hindrances that serve to prevent churches from cooperating on this level.

Accordingly, interested Church leaders should begin to prepare themselves. Again, they can reflect back on Nneka's story for some insight regarding this suggestion. The arrangements for Nneka's husband *finally* fell into place at the church facilities where she took Pastor Daniel, but not without some hard fought and gut-level determination of sheer faith on her part. Hopefully, our situations will not be as dramatic as Nneka's.

It would be to the advantage of Christian church leaders to seriously consider their responsibility to advance this dimension by the use of their facilities. It may only be a matter of time until a grieving individual shows up at our church seeking this type of ministry. Hopefully, we will be prepared to accommodate them.

HOME GROUPS

The author has discovered by experience that home groups are another viable avenue through which individuals can receive quality training and impartation of this dimension. The ongoing quality of dialogue and discussion that abounds in small groups elicits even more revelation to continue unfolding on this subject. Also, working relationships become established with this purpose in mind. This will enable a core group of individuals to rise up, and who will avail themselves for team minstry.

This setting is perhaps the wisest approach for initially releasing and imparting the truths of this message until our affiliated religious institutions have the eyes of their understanding illuminated on this subject. Who we invite and how we invite other individuals should also be done in a wise and prudent manner.

MENTOR PROGRAMS

One advisable way to advance this dimension with some much needed oversight and accountability is through the establishment of mentor programs. Natural and spiritual progress of mentorees can be formally taught, trained and released. We know about being taught and trained through classroom settings. There's only one other way to be taught and trained when it comes to raising the dead, and that is by doing.

Evidence of this type of training can be seen in the Old Testament of the Bible as well as in the New. In the Old Testament, Prophet Elisha first sent forth his willing servant, Gehazi, to minister to the Shunnamite woman's deceased son. Gehazi was given the opportunity to go minister to this boy until Elisha could get himself together to make the trip. The experience had to be invaluable for Gehazi even though he was unsuccessful.

The point being made is that Gehazi was evidently ready and willing to step out in this fashion aside from Elisha. He had probably been prepared as much as he could by Elisha for this purpose. This is one further reason we should consider establishing some *Gehazi gatherings* of our own. We can reproduce ourselves into others so they can be prepared for the opportunity to be released for ministry in this capacity when we are not readily available.

As for the New Testament, the Scriptures reveal that disciples usually accompanied Jesus when He was ministering to deceased individuals. These individuals were afforded a bird's eye view of how to go about exercising their faith for the same. They were able to learn a few lessons from their own in the process.

For instance, the disciples who accompanied Jesus to Jairus' house learned one invaluable lesson for sure (Matthew 9:19). They learned about how to stand and believe God in the face of unbelieving and unruly individuals, and not be sidetracked. More was *caught* than could have ever been *taught* simply by observing Jesus in action.

We can see that mentor relationships which provide for teaching, as well as hands on observation and training, would be in keeping with the Scriptures. Not only are we called to be hearers, but we are called to be doers of the Word as well. A good hands-on mentor relationship enables believers to become both. This atmosphere will have people in place and ready to minister when someone dies a premature death.

THE BASE COVERED

God still has the base covered regardless of whether leaders of home groups, churches, denominations, networks, Bible colleges or training centers choose to gravitate toward this subject. As we will see, the responsibility to see that this message is ushered into the earth rests upon the governmental and foundational offices of the Church.

CHAPTER FIFTEEN

~

AN APOSTOLIC MANDATE

*"Go therefore and make disciples of all the nations,
baptizing them in the name of the Father and of
the Son and of the Holy Spirit, teaching them to
observe all things that I have commanded you;*
Matthew 28:19-20a

Hopefully, you have observed that the words "apostle" and "prophet" continues to become more commonplace among Christian circles today. This, of course, depends on your overall exposure to the church world. I was raised in a traditional and denominational church for the first eighteen years of my life. These two offices were regarded by this denomination as having existed in the early Church but not for today. As a result, the ingrained tendency existed to automatically dismiss those who had the *audacity* to be using these two words. Believers who took on the use of these two words were automatically regarded as *false prophets* or *false apostles*.

163

It was not until my mid-twenties that I began to realize the waywardness of my indoctrination. I gradually began to see and better understand what God was doing on earth in the way of building His Church, and how modern day apostles and prophets play a key role in this building process. You will too as you continue reading.

We will continue moving forward upon the assumption that the reader is well aware of the thousands of apostles and prophets at work in the Church today throughout the earth. This chapter will discuss their fundamental role and function strictly in keeping with the expectation that they supernaturally demonstrate the power of God. Demonstrating the power of God is core to the apostolic when viewed in the light of how Jesus very first and specifically mandated apostles to function, especially when it comes to raising the dead.

As we will see, apostles and prophets have the shared responsibility in seeing that this practice is restored and integrated into Christian culture once again.

WHAT ARE APOSTLES?

Fundamentally speaking, apostles are those individuals upon whom the foundation of the Church is built. God first appointed apostles in the Church to help equip the saints for the work of the ministry. This truth is gleaned from three Scriptures; Ephesians 2:20, 1 Corinthians 12:28 and Ephesians 4:11.

Ephesians 2:20 states that, *"the foundation of the Church is built upon apostles and prophets, with Christ Jesus being the Chief cornerstone."* I Corinthians 12:28 states, *"And God has appointed these in the church: first apostles, second prophets, third teachers, after that miracles, then gifts of healing, helps, administrations, varieties of tongues."*

Further, Ephesians 4:11-12 states that, *"He Himself* (Jesus) *gave some to be apostles, some prophets, some evangelists, and some pastors and teachers for the equipping of the saints for the work of ministry, for the edifying of the Body of Christ.* The corporate Church at large is familiar with the evangelists, pastors and teachers, but not that of apostles and prophets. Nevertheless, apostles and prophets have begun to visibly emerge on the scene and take their rightful place.

Many believers think that these two offices ceased with the death of the original twelve apostles. Not so. The twelve apostles were called to be an example and demonstration of God's intended biblical pattern for future apostolic ministry. God would not dangle His intended biblical pattern before us and then tell us we could not duplicate this pattern because these twelve human beings died.

In fact, the reader can find that there were over twenty apostles mentioned in the New Testament, one being a woman. This ministry office had already begun to reproduce and multiply through other individuals before these twelve men died. Remember, God gave five offices in which to equip the saints and this is one of them. God is once again restoring the foundation of the Church that He is building in the earth today.

We have looked at the fundamental purpose of apostles within the Church. Now let's look at one aspect of how they are expected to function.

AN APOSTOLIC MANDATE

Matthew 10:1-8 provides a very succinct and fundamental mandate of how Jesus expected apostles to function in the way of the supernatural power of God. This passage of Scripture occurred when Jesus called His twelve disciples together for the purpose of "sending" them out into ministry. Notice how the reference to these disciples changes from verse one to verse two.

[1]*"And when He had called His twelve **disciples** to Him, He gave them **power** over unclean spirits, to cast them out, and to heal all kinds of sickness and all kinds of disease.*

> ²*Now the names of the twelve* **apostles** *are these..."*

Verse one refers to these men as *disciples*. Verse two refers to them as *apostles*. They are now being called apostles. Something transpires between verses one and two that now qualifies them being called apostles.

Note in verse one that after Jesus called them together that He gave them *power*. We see that the first action Jesus took toward commissioning these disciples was that of *imparting* power to them. They were referred to as *apostles* after this happened. The difference in being called apostles, as opposed to disciples, was the power of God being imparted into their lives as the apostolic mantle was bestowed upon them.

Jesus continued to address these twelve men after conferring the mantle of an apostle upon them. It quickly becomes apparent in verses seven through eight why this *power* was much needed. He was about to let them know His fundamental and basic expectations of them as apostles.

Matthew 10:7-8 tells us that Jesus *"sent out and commanded"* them saying:

> ⁷*"And as you go, preach, saying, 'The kingdom of heaven is at hand.*
> ⁸*Heal the sick, cleanse the lepers,* **raise the dead**, *cast out demons."*

Notice that these four directives were given in the form of a command. No option existed. The choice had clearly been made for them by Jesus.

Jesus gave a clear and simple mandate by saying, *"Heal the sick, cleanse the lepers, raise the dead, and cast out demons..."* We can therefore deduce that the basic and fundamental responsibility of a true apostle is to function and operate in all four aspects of this mandate. Clearly, this mandate is inclusive of raising the dead.

APOSTLES TODAY

Jesus expects His apostles to operate in the power of God now just as they did in the Early Church days. He expects those called as apostles to heal the sick, cleanse the lepers, cast out demons and raise the dead no matter what type of an apostle they claim to be. Let's define what an apostle is for the sake of definition.

According to this author, the best all-inclusive and working definition of an apostle today is found in Peter Wagner's book, *Spheres of Authority*. Wagner's definition is this: "An apostle is a Christian leader, gifted, taught, commissioned, and sent by God with the authority to establish the foundational government of the church within an assigned sphere of ministry by hearing what the Spirit is saying to the churches and by setting things in order accordingly for the growth and maturity of the church."[1]

Hone in on one particular part of this definition: "...and by setting things in order accordingly... ." Not only do things need to be set in order in the natural, but they need to be set in order in the way of the supernatural as well. Apostolically speaking, the time has come for the natural and supernatural aspects of raising the dead to be set in order in the Church today.

The natural assignment of apostles will vary from locale to locale, region to region, and nation to nation. Given the ruling principalities over a particular geographical area, these assignments will elicit varying degrees of different supernatural functions and strengths from different apostles. One thing should remain core and central no matter

---

1. Wagner, C. Peter, *Spheres of Authority*, (Wagner Publications), 2002, p. 27.

what function an apostle carries out in a particular geographical area. There is a directive to carry out all four aspects of this mandate at the core of apostolic commissioning!

Functioning in these four aspects of ministry has been determined for you by Jesus if you call yourself an apostle. Look around and take note if the apostles you observe or come into contact with function in these capacities. A good possibility exist that new territories and spheres of authority will have to be charted in the natural and spiritual realm when it comes to raising the dead.

This should not be construed to mean that those around you are not true apostles whether they are or are not yet raising the dead. It just means that there is some maturing to do. Remember, Jesus called His disciples apostles before they were sent out and ever did one miracle, but they knew what was expected of them.

Apostles of today should know that Jesus expects them to raise the dead as well.

RAISING THE DEAD

The directive to raise the dead has yet to be demonstrated and taught in the Body of Christ like the other three directives have. Why? Why has this dimension of the apostolic eluded the thinking and writing of major apostolic leaders and scholars within the Body of Christ? If anyone was going to be demonstrating and releasing revelation on this aspect of the apostolic, they would. But why hasn't the revelation of this particular aspect of this apostolic mandate come to the forefront within the corporate Body of Christ?

We should first remember that revelation is given to us for the building of the Church. God said, He "will build" His Church. Matthew 16:18 states, "*And I also say to you that you are Peter, and on this rock (of revelation) I will build My church...*". "Will build" lets us know that God is progressively building His corporate Church. It will be built upon revelation given to various individuals.

When God begins to corporately release further revelation in order to continue the building process, it is because the Church is ready for the next building block of information. One reason the message of Christians raising the dead is coming to the forefront of the Church in corporate fashion is because the Body of Christ is ready. All five-fold governmental gifts according to Ephesians 4:11-12 have now been restored to the Church.

Healing the sick, cleansing the lepers, and casting out demons have served a purpose of preparing and equipping the Body of Christ to apprehend the enemies of sickness and disease. Now we will begin approaching the enemy of death in this same manner. God has not left us in the dark on this directive to raise the dead any more than He did the other three directives of this apostolic mandate. He just waited a little bit longer to corportely release the necessary revelation for "how to" go about ministering in this capacity.

Simply stated, the timing of God in releasing progressive revelation upon which to further build His Church comes at His will and discretion, not ours. God is God. He has His unique way of upholding the eyes of our spiritual enlightenment, regardless of who we may be, until He is ready for revelation to be *corporately* released and the Church is ready to receive it.

This author submits that now is the time for the corporate release of this revelation within the Body of Christ, especially beginning with apostles. And, it should begin to be released through prophets as well.

WHAT ABOUT PROPHETS?

We earlier stated in Ephesians 2:20 that, *"the foundation of the Church is built upon apostles **and prophets**, ...".* Prophets comprise as much of the foundational makeup of the Church as apostles. With this in mind, the vital role of prophets cannot be overlooked where raising the dead is concerned. It stands to reason that prophets have a responsibility to restore this dimension side-by-side with apostles.

169

Amos 3:7 states that, "*Surely the Lord God does nothing unless He reveals His secret to His servants the prophets.*" God reveals to prophets what He wants done in the earth. The role of the prophet had just as much to do with the releasing of this particular mandate to the apostles as the mandate itself. This mandate was released by Jesus, our Prophet, Priest and King.

Jesus also availed Himself in death situations and raised deceased individuals. Those who profess to be prophets today should take Jesus as their example. What goes for apostles in the way of raising the dead also goes for prophets. Apostles and prophets, being the foundational offices of the church, have the shared responsibility to carry out all four directives of this mandate.

SPEARHEADING THIS DIMENSION

Jesus not only called apostles and prophets to raise the dead, but also pinpointed others called *believers* to do these greater works. Apostles and prophets are believers; however, not all believers are apostles or prophets. Fundamentally speaking, the basic expectation for a believer or an apostle or prophet to raise the dead is to exercise actions of faith. Beyond this expectation is one distinguishing characteristic that sets these two groups apart from each other.

The decision for apostles and prophets to raise the dead has already been mandated for them by Jesus. They do not have a choice but to accept this mandate now. Believers, on the other hand, have a choice to make as to *when* they will embrace this dimension.

We earlier established that Jesus *commanded* apostles and prophets to raise the dead. He also left them with what has been coined the Great Commission in Matthew 28:19-20. They were told to make disciples of all the nations, and were instructed to *teach* disciples to do *all things* that Jesus had *commanded* apostles to do.

We know from Matthew 10:5 and 8, that Jesus *commanded* His apostles to heal the sick, raise the dead, cleanse the lepers and cast out demons. Jesus also provided a very real example for how to do this when He walked upon the earth with them. Today, He also left us with a good example as well — His Word, the Holy Bible.

Again, John 14:12 states, *"Most assuredly, I say to you, he who believes in Me, the works that I do he will do also; and greater works than these he will do..."*. It is the God-given duty of apostles and prophets to spearhead this dimension of raising the dead within the corporate Body of Christ. They are to see that believers are taught and trained to do the *works* and *greater works* Jesus did. This is inclusive of raising the dead.

The fact that apostles and prophets have been chosen by God to teach and demonstrate this mandate does not make them any better than disciples or believers. It just merely reinforces the five-fold governmental expectation for functioning in this capacity. *Anyone* can raise the dead when biblical actions of faith are appropriately exercised before God.

RESURRECTION MINISTRIES

Considered by this author to be a modern day forerunner of this dimension is a resurrection minister by the name of David Hogan. He is responsible for the oversight of a ministry called Freedom Ministries, based in Mexico. Additionally, he works with approximately 28 Indian tribes in the mountains of Central America, and has approximately 600 churches that relate to his ministry.

Over three hundred confirmed cases where deceased individuals were raised had taken place within his ministry at the time this information was obtained.[1] Hogan was personally responsible for

---

1. May 2, 2004, Ministry by David Hogan, Fishers of Men Ministries, Ft. Walton Beach, FL.

approximately 25 of these resurrections. Truly, this ministry can be regarded as an epicenter for activity in this regard.

Curry Blake, who was given legal rights to continue the legacy of the John G. Lake Ministries, stands out as another credible minister of resurrection life (www.jglm.org). Seven deceased individuals had been resurrected under his ministry at the time this information was obtained.[2] These are two ministers that the author has personally seen and heard reference these facts.

One only needs to browse through the ministry website of Rolland and Heidi Baker to see the tremendous work that these two Americans have pioneered (www.irismin.org). Iris Ministries, Inc. is the official name of their ministry. They are based out of Pemba, Cabo Delgado, Mozambique, and minister among the poorest of the poor. Several have been raised from the dead within the scope of their ministerial influence at the time of this writing.

The reality has already become apparent within these ministries, and others not mentioned, that individuals should be ministered to whether they are sick, diseased, oppressed, or deceased.

THE CHOICE

Obvious to the natural eye is the fact that raising the dead has yet to be visibly restored within the corporate Church of today like it is going to be. Time will truly become our friend in the process. Prophets have been echoing on a more frequent basis that now is the time for the dead to start being raised. The time is literally here and now for this declaration to start becoming a reality.

Earthly resurrections will begin to escalate as apostles and prophets make the choice to begin pioneering this dimension.

---

2. February 11, 2005, Ministry by Curry Blake, Christian International Family Church, Santa Rosa Beach, FL.

CHAPTER SIXTEEN

~

HIS FOOTSTOOL

*"And God both raised up the Lord and will also
raise us up by His power."*

1 Corinthians 6:14

Do you ever cease to be amazed at all the credit God gets when
things like calamities, earthquakes and hurricanes happen? These
happenings are usually referred to as *acts of God*, especially within the
language of most insurance policies. God usually gets the blame for
all the deaths instead of the blame being placed where it should be —
on the devil. Nevertheless, the fault always falls back on God because
He *could have prevented* such bad things from happening.

God also could have stretched forth His Hand and prevented
His own Son, Jesus, from being crucified on the cross, but He did
not. He allowed Jesus to go to the cross for a purpose. Through it,
mankind was given the opportunity to be redeemed from having to
live with such evil eternally, after we die. If we believe on the Lord

Jesus Christ we will have everlasting life in heaven, instead of everlasting death in hell.

Consider the powerful things that will first have to take place within the corporate Body of Christ before Jesus can come back and forever redeem us from this world's present evils. We know that all the enemies of Jesus will have to be put under His feet and made His footstool.

DEATH HIS FOOTSTOOL

Hebrews 10:12-13 states, *"But this Man (Jesus), after He had offered one sacrifice for sins forever, sat down at the right hand of God, from that time waiting till His enemies are made His footstool.* Matthew 22:44 states it this way: *"Sit at My (God) right hand, till I make Your enemies Your footstool."* God said that He was going to make Jesus' enemies the footstool of Jesus.

The Old Testament and New Testament clearly indicates what is the footstool of Jesus. The Lord states in Isaiah 66:1 that *"Heaven is My throne, And earth is My footstool.* Acts 7:49 reiterates this same fact that *"Heaven is My throne, And earth is My footstool."* In essence, it appears as if we have two uses of the word footstool: His enemies *being* made His footstool and the fact that the earth *is* His footstool.

For the sake of clarity, a distinction between the two uses of this word should be made. As you can see, the earth is explicitly stated as *the* footstool of Jesus, but the enemies of God are to *become* His footstool. The enemies will become an integral part of this footstool when they are brought into subjection by God through the Body of Christ.

Jesus walked upon the earth and brought into subjection every enemy known to man. He *"put all things in subjection under his feet. For in that he put all in subjection under him He left nothing that is not put under him".* If Jesus left nothing to be put under His feet, this means that death was put under His feet (Hebrews 2:8).

According to the Greek word, "hupotasso," the word "subjection" used here means to "subdue." This definition is in keeping with the original mandate God first gave man in Genesis 1:28. God told man to "subdue" the earth, and nothing has changed. This mandate is still in effect.

As Hebrew 2:8 goes on to say, "*...But now we do not yet see all things put under him*". We do not *yet* see all things put under the feet of Jesus in the earth. This is because we, the Body of Christ, have *yet* to subdue them. The Body of Christ is expected to function like its Head, Jesus Christ.

Jesus Christ already overcame His enemies in the earth and is seated at the right hand of God. Corporately speaking, the Body of Christ has yet to subdue His enemies. This is one main reason why we are still here on earth and not with Him in heaven. When these enemies are subdued by the Body of Christ and put under His feet they will become His footstool. Jesus has to stay seated at the right hand of God until this happens.

The one enemy that has eluded the authority and dominion of the Body of Christ most is the enemy of death. 1 Corinthians 15:26 states that "*the last enemy that will be destroyed is death*." The focus of this verse should be on the fact the Bible affirms that death is an enemy. It stands to reason that if death is an enemy of Jesus then it is an enemy of the Body of Christ on this earth also. This enemy has to be made His footstool.

One of God's ways in seeing that the enemy of death becomes the footstool of Jesus is inclusive of the earthly Church operating in the power of God to raise the dead. In other words, the Church should be confronting and overcoming the spirit of death that is unleashed prematurely over individuals in the earth today.

OVERCOMING DEATH
The Body of Christ should grasp and understand one concept in

particular about overcoming death. Overcoming death is a continual process for the Body of Christ. Jesus instantly overcame death for us when He died on the cross and was subsequently resurrected by the power of God. The Body of Christ is to continue overcoming death until Jesus returns. God did not leave us powerless against death either. He made a provision for us to receive this power.

Acts 1:2-3 states that, He came back to earth and was seen forty days by the apostles before He finally ascended. During this time, Acts 1:4 states that Jesus Christ *commanded* His apostles to stay in Jerusalem and wait for the Promise of the Holy Spirit. We know that He had given power to the apostles in Matthew 10:1-2, but now they would need the Holy Spirit's power since Jesus would be leaving. This is why He told them to tarry in Jerusalem and wait. He told them that *"you shall receive power when the Holy Spirit has come upon you"* *(Acts 1:8).*

The apostles were filled with power and an unknown tongue sat upon each of them, and the others with them, as the Holy Spirit was unleashed in the earth on the day of Pentecost. This same Holy Spirit still dwells within God's people today, and is waiting to unleash this same power and an unknown tongue upon them as well when they are ready to receive it. This is the power of the Holy Spirit that enables us to do the greater works that Jesus said we would do. It is through this power that we are to raise the dead and overcome death in the land.

We are to continue overcoming death's grip in the earth that Jesus overcame in Hell. The power of death could not keep Jesus confined to His *hell in Hell* when He overcame and prevailed against it, as evidenced by His resurrection. Death will not be able to keep the Body of Christ confined to Her hell of sickness, poverty and death in the earth as we begin to overcome and prevail in the earth.

What Jesus did in hell when He overcame and prevailed over death was only the beginning of the end of death. The Church is to continue overcoming it in the earth. God will destroy it in the end (1 Corinthians 15:26; Revelations 20:14). Like John, the Revelator stated in Revelation 21:4, *"there shall be no more death"* for those who believe in Jesus Christ as the Son of the living God. All things will be made new for us (Revelation 21:5).

THE LAST DAYS

The term *last days* is not new to the Body of Christ. The phrase, "we are living in the last days" has been trumpeted in Christian circles for years. How accurate are we on a specific and literal basis when we say "last days"? No man really knows, however, how we can gain an even clearer perspective on this phrase with regard to the subject at hand.

The Scripture states in 2 Peter 3:8 that *"a day with the Lord is as a thousand years."* One could deduce from this verse that the Church is in Her third day since two thousand years have now come and gone. It becomes apparent that there is an unfolding parallel between Jesus overcoming death while in Hell and the Church overcoming death while in the earth.

Jesus overcame hell on the third day. It now appears that the Church will overcome and prevail over death in Her third day as well. If this third day parallel holds true to course, it looks as if death will also be the final enemy for us to overcome like it was for Jesus. With this in mind, we might want to think twice before we begin trumpeting that "Jesus is coming soon."

We might be living in the Third Day but remember that the day is very young. There is much more work to be done by the saints in preparing to overcome and prevail over this enemy called death. If we truly believe we are living in the "last days," we should work like we really are in them. We should start preparing to raise the dead so that the enemy of death becomes His footstool within the earth.

NEW LEVELS

Prophetically speaking, God is now releasing the revelation for how to go about raising the dead. There's nothing really new about Christians raising the dead except for the fact that it has not been openly practiced within the Church for centuries. He is leading the Body of Christ, especially apostles and prophets, to begin unearthing and resurrecting this old facet of Christianity once again.

The *present truth* Church of today will insure that raising the dead is once again restored and openly practiced. Jesus openly practiced raising the dead. He expects believers who will do the greater works to do the same. God is allowing resurrection revelation to be released in a corporate fashion so that the overcoming and prevailing earthly Church will culminate with the enemy of death being put under the feet of Jesus.

This resurrection anointing is now being corporately realized once again. This anointing will begin to pervade the foundation of the Body of Christ. In the process, God is once again leading the corporate Church into a deeper level and greater dimension of the power of His Spirit. However, as the old saying goes, new levels are usually accompanied by new devils.

Should we decide to take a stance against this enemy then we should equip ourselves to deal with the possible repercussions. Frankly speaking, we should not miscalculate the potential backlash that could be directed at our families and friends. Having said this, solidify the contents of this text not only within your heart, but see to it that family and friends become settled and secured in this message as well.

The Body of Christ should no longer be viewed by the devil as helpless and hopeless sitting ducks whenever and wherever premature assignments of death decide to rest. Death has prevailed over the saints of God long enough. Now is the time for this role to begin reversing. It is the *kairos* time for the corporate Church to come forth and overcome the spirit of death.

This is the overcoming and prevailing Church actively at work.

OVERCOMING AND PREVAILING

The Church has come a long way in the last 2000 years. Nevertheless, there is still plenty of work to be done before Jesus can be released from the Right Hand of God. This is especially true when it come to raising the dead. The Body of Christ will have to do more than scratch the surface of this dimension.

Setting the corporate wheels of resurrection life into motion to begin overcoming death will take some time for believers in the Body of Christ to accomplish. Nevertheless, it will be done! We know that the enemy of death has to be made Jesus' footstool before He can be released from His sitting. This fact leads to one ultimate question that is of interest to us all.

To what degree will the corporate Church have to be overcoming and prevailing upon this enemy of death before God will consider it the footstool of Jesus? When we figure out what God's full definition of the word *overcoming* is, we may have a further clue to this question. Attempts to answer this question would be pure speculation at this point.

Matthew 24:36 tells us that, *"But of that day and hour no one know, not even the angels of heaven, but my Father only."* Only God knows when Jesus will be released from sitting at God's Right Hand. What we do know is that the sooner apostles and prophets take their rightful place to spearhead the dimension of believers raising the dead, the sooner He can return. Further, the sooner believers accept the prophetic directive from Jesus to step out and do the greater works in this manner, the sooner He can return.

OUR GAUGE FOR HIS RETURN

Believers in Jesus Christ earnestly long to know when Jesus is coming back. Many worldwide events and happenings are now being construed as indicators of the end time and His return. Revelation from heaven has been given to many different individuals to be able to show how different events and happenings fit into the *end time* plan of God — however long *end time* means.

God's people can look to the unfolding and continuing events pertaining to Israel as an indicator. We can also see that the cup of iniquity in the earth looks to be getting *full*. Wars and rumors of wars are taking place. Nations are rising against nations. These events and many others can all have the definition of *end times* attached to them. They are being used by many as a gauge for assessing that Jesus will come back soon.

Much of this information is intriguing and very interesting to know. In fact, many continue to trumpet Jesus' coming as imminent, or that He is coming *soon* based on these worldwide events. But, before we grab such statements and run with them, we should consider the following for a moment. Perhaps we should remain centrally focused on the progress of the mature Church that He is coming back for as a primary gauge for His return.

First, look around and see what is taking place within the corporate Church that God is building. No one with the mind of Christ can deny that many signs, wonders and miracles are taking place today. Many souls are coming to Jesus. People are being healed from their sicknesses and diseases. Demons are being cast out through the many deliverance ministries in the earth today.

We should rejoice and continue to give God glory in the midst of all these signs, wonders and miracles. However, we know for sure that one strength is still visibly lacking within the corporate Body of Christ. It is that of subduing the enemy of death. The spirit of death prematurely resting over individuals, not to mention (in this writing) over worldwide geographical regions, still need to be confronted and addressed in God's earth today!

HASTEN HIS COMING

Regardless of any unfolding event destined to occur in the earth, one thing is for certain. Jesus is seated in the Throne Room of Heaven at the Right Hand of God until all enemies, including the enemy of death, are made His footstool by the power of the Holy Spirit of God operating through the Body of Christ. When we begin to see a corporate escalation of earthly resurrections happening among the corporate Body of Christ, believing saints of God can begin to trumpet with even more confidence that the Lord is coming soon!

2 Peter 3:12 states that, believers should be *"looking for and hastening the coming of the day of God."* It stands to reason that, if believers can hasten the coming of the Lord then they can delay His return. The choice not to embrace this spiritual dimension, for whatever seemingly valid reason we may have, delays the coming of the Lord.

Perhaps you have already found yourself in one of these situations with your deceased loved one who was not raised. And, the thought of going back into one of these situations is too much of a grim reminder of the past. This is an understandable and viable reason during an obvious season of grief, but not for the duration. In order to understand this stance, let's keep perspective of the bigger picture for why we are even here on this earth.

We have been put here on this earth to prepare the way for the second coming of our Lord, Jesus Christ. Preparing the way of the Lord is not always pleasant or pain free. Our personal hurts and pains are very real, especially the experience of losing a loved one. I know. I lost my dad, granddad and step-dad all within a five month period when I was eighteen years old. However, painful experiences like these should not forever override Jesus' *prophetic declaration* and *command* to us to do the greater works such as raise the dead.

The point being made here is that a lack of support and participation, based on our own personal resurrection experiences of loved ones who were not raised, only delays the second coming of

Jesus. A decision to withdraw and refrain from approaching the enemy of death is exactly what the devil wants. This is just one example of a seemingly justifiable strategy that the enemy will attempt to impose in order to delay the coming of the Lord in these last days. Strategies like these prolongs Satan's time here on earth and delays Jesus' return.

For this reason alone, the Body of Christ should accept the role and responsibility to confront this enemy called death on every existing front known to us. This is part of our spiritual heritage as true believers and followers of Jesus Christ. The following words used by Paul E. Billheimer in his book, *Don't Waste Your Sorrows*, can be aptly utilized to sum up believers' rights to raise the dead.

> *"...there is a legal basis for full deliverance in this life from every result of the Fall for every child of God."*[1]

Church! It is time to come forth and usher in the preparation and restoration of Christian believers raising the dead in the earth today like never before!

---

1. Dr. Bill Hamon, *The Eternal Church*, Destiny Image Publishers, Shippensburg, PA, Revised Edition 2003, p. 306.

SECTION TWO:

CORPORATE AND THEOLOGICAL CONSIDERATIONS

Section One addressed the individual and practical aspects of Christians preparing to raise the dead. The contents of this next section are more corporate in scope. Since God is still in the process of building the Church that will prevail, He is still speaking to the Church. May we, as individuals, have an ear to hear what God is saying to the Church in a corporate regard.

The Holy Spirit of God is corporately brooding over the Church once again in that the Body of Christ is being ushered into a resurrection season. The corporate mentality of the Church in approaching death in this new season will have to be updated into present truth about dying and death. The ability of the Body of Christ to successfully transition into this resurrection season will require a total paradigm shift in our way of thinking when someone dies.

We will be able to see more clearly what God is doing in the Church with regard to raising the dead as we look at this subject through the eyes of restoration. The bigger picture of why Christians are expected to raise the dead will begin to come alive even more. We will see why this resurrection anointing is now beginning to be released to the Body of Christ in corporate fashion. A fundamental picture of how the frequent occurrence of earthly resurrections fit into the grand scheme of God's overall plan for the resurrected Body of Christ will also become much clearer.

My objective in presenting this section is to further encourage and embolden the Body of Christ to set their sights on entering into the dimension of raising the dead so Jesus Christ can return.

PART FOUR:

RESURRECTION RESTORATION

~

CHAPTER SEVENTEEN

HELP OUR UNBELIEF

"I will not be negligent to remind you always
of these things, though you know and are
established in the present truth."

I Peter 1:12

A major key for the Body of Christ to begin raising the dead is the ability to recognize and move beyond the residing corporate mentality by which we may presently abide. Whether we are aware of it or not, our present belief system may not necessarily reflect the present truth of what God has revealed when it comes to raising the dead. God's desire is for this area of belief to be challenged, changed and updated.

Our own unbelief can be difficult for us to realize and identify at times. This is especially true when it comes to raising the dead. Mary and Martha were prime examples of this fact when Lazarus died. Interestingly enough, the same issues of unbelief that Mary and Martha could not realize are analogous to the existing mentality that tends to be resident within the Body of Christ.

Jesus deemed it important enough to stop and address their respective issues of unbelief. The Body of Christ would also benefit from taking a closer look at these issues. They will provide us with some insight that could help pinpoint any possible and pre-existing unbelief by which we may also unknowingly abide.

As we will see, an update and major shift in our way of thinking about raising the dead may be necessary. These same issues that are unknowingly resident within the Body of Christ may have to be rectified as well.

JESUS WAS SUMMONED

It is important to keep one fact in mind as the discussion of Mary and Martha's issues unfold. These sisters did not have Jesus summoned for the purpose of raising Lazarus from the dead. John 11:1-4 states that *"...the sisters sent to Him, saying, "Lord, behold, he whom you love is sick."* They summoned Jesus because Lazarus was very sick, not because they were expecting Him to come and raise Lazarus from the dead.

Mary and Martha's faith was for Jesus to come minister healing to Lazarus so he would not die. Jesus eventually came two days later but Lazarus had already died before He got there. When He did arrive, Jesus could have requested to immediately be taken to the grave site of Lazarus. He did not. He first deemed it important to talk to these two sisters about issues that are also relevant to us today.

Jesus had two individual and separate conversations with Martha and Mary about the death of Lazarus. Their unrealized unbelief was revealed within the heart of these two, brief discussions with Jesus. Consequently, they were challenged to confront their issues of unbelief about dying, death and earthly resurrections.

MARY'S ISSUE

Mary was like many of us today in these situations. She had a difficult time coming to grips with the death of Lazarus. She did not even run out to meet Jesus when He arrived on the scene like Martha did. Grief had gripped her soul to the point that Martha had to *secretly* go tell her, *The Teacher* was here and was calling for her.

In verse 32 of John 11, *"when Mary came to where Jesus was, and saw Him, she fell down at His feet, saying to Him, "Lord, if You had been here, my brother would not have died."* Catch the essence of this statement. Evident is the fact that she only believed Jesus to heal Lazarus from a dying bed but not raise him from a bed of death.

Like the majority of Christians today, Mary was expecting Jesus to come on the scene so her loved one would not die. She truly believed Jesus could raise Lazarus when he was dying, but believed the earthly life of Lazarus was over since that did not happen. The thought of him being raised from the dead when Jesus arrived did not enter her mind! Does this belief system of Mary's sound familiar to us?

We pray and pray and pray for someone when they are dying. When they die, we cease to continue ministering life to them. Have we ever attempted to minister resurrection life, or allowed anyone else to minister life over our deceased loved one after they prematurely died? Or, did we follow through with the conventional response of planning a funeral or burial without the thought of any further intervention? Our answer to these questions should provide us with somewhat of a barometer for our present level of belief.

Mary, and those surrounding her, could only believe Jesus had the power to keep someone from dying. Jesus had already told Martha when He first arrived on the scene that, *"Your brother will rise again."* Jesus knew Lazarus was going to be raised back to life. Yet Mary, the one who was content to sit at Jesus' feet, could not spiritually comprehend that He had the power to raise Lazarus from the dead. She could only believe Him to raise Lazarus from his dying bed.

Jesus had spent much time teaching, eating, and fellowshiping at Mary and Martha's house. A close and personal relationship with them and Lazarus had been developed. Despite Mary's quality exposure and proximity to the personal ministry of Jesus, she was still spiritually unaware of the realistic possibility of Lazarus being raised from the dead by Jesus.

Likewise, the Body of Christ today has sat at the feet of Jesus, practiced His presence through high praise, and entered into intense times of prayer and intercession. We have even prayed for the sick to be healed, demons to be cast out in the name of Jesus, and prophesied the word of the Lord, all the while seeing miracles, signs and wonders. We have done all these things to experience tangible manifestation of the presence of God.

There is no better place to be than in the presence of God — as long as we are advancing in the power of the Holy Spirit. Yet, if the only action being considered after a loved one dies is that of the preparation and planning for a funeral or burial, we need to update our belief system where raising the dead is concerned. This is exactly the same kind of unbelief that Mary had to realize. But, let's try to get into Mary's world in case we are tempted to criticize her for her unbelief.

We should ask ourselves one question. Would we have been able to believe for Lazarus to be raised anymore than Mary if our deceased loved one had already been dead for four days and already in their grave? Realistically, would we have allowed a mature believer to go to the grave site and have the physical barriers removed from the grave, in order to command life to return to the deceased? This is an example of the barriers of unbelief that the Body of Christ will have to overcome in order to prevail upon the enemy of death.

Put yourself in Mary's shoes and ask yourself this question: To what extent would you have allowed any further ministry to take place over Lazarus after he died? The extent of Mary's belief system stopped short of believing that God can raise someone from the dead. This belief system was borne out in her words and ensuing actions. In short, she stopped at the point of believing God to raise someone when they are dying and not when they are dead.

Generally speaking, Mary's issue of unbelief personifies the height of corporate faith levels that tend to reside within the Body of Christ. Consideration should be given to the updating of the corporate belief system of the Church in this regard now that the limitations of this type of belief system have been presented. It should begin to be updated from an existing level of *dying persons healed* to that of *dead persons being raised.*

This update reflects the fact that we can believe God to raise someone from a dying bed as well as from a bona fide state of death when the necessary and unconventional actions of faith are wisely exercised by faith-filled believers.

MARTHA'S ISSUE

Martha encountered Jesus before Mary did. John 11:21-30 lets us know that she ran out to meet Him as He was arriving. Her first statement to Him was, *"Lord, if you had been here, my brother would not have died."* Like Mary, she was expecting Jesus to arrive so Lazarus would not die, but Martha's response was expressed with even further insight and thought.

Martha went on to say in John 11:22, *"But even now I know that whatever You ask of God, God will give You."* Unlike Mary, Martha responded by leaving the door open and saying *"whatever."* She knew God would do *whatever* Jesus asked Him to do. She continued on by further conveying to Jesus in John 11:24 that she knew Lazarus would *"rise again in the resurrection at the last day."*

Martha was applying her own limited definition of what she perceived the word *resurrection* to mean. She was referring to the point in the end time where the saints of God will be raised and, those who are alive, will be translated to meet Jesus in the clouds. Martha's futuristic use of this term was not what Jesus was trying to convey when using the word resurrection.

Jesus promptly replied in John 11:25 by saying *"I am the resurrection, and the life;..."* In other words, Jesus was trying to convey to Martha that earthly resurrections are possible for the here and now. *"I am"* is present tense. The necessity existed for Jesus to clarify and make a distinction about Martha's mentality and present use of the word *resurrection*.

The word *resurrection* can, and should be, freely used in dual fashion without hesitation. It can be used to mean the resurrection of the saints of God in the end time. Or, the word can be used to mean an earthly resurrection of someone literally being raised from the dead in this present time. Jesus was conveying the latter meaning of this word to Martha. Her limited mentality of this word's definition was preventing her from seeing the intended and deeper meaning of it for the present.

This same mentality that Martha exhibited regarding the use of the word "resurrection" is the mentality that will need to be addressed within the Body of Christ today. Believers should not only keep waiting and looking for the resurrection power of God to begin at the end of the earthly Church Age in order to raise individuals. The literal resurrection power of God begins with believers learning how to raise the dead and demonstrate this resurrection power in the earth today.

The tendency to only feel the freedom to use the word *resurrection* when referring to Jesus' resurrection, or using it only in the sense of expecting end-time resurrection, can be partially attributed to our overlooking the present tense application of earthly resurrections today. This is a restraint and oversight that the Body of Christ will have to move past. As a result, the use of the word *resurrection* will become much more commonplace.

The full comprehension of Martha's oversight of Lazarus being resurrected in this earthly life was more fully realized after Jesus called him forth from his tomb of death. The Body of Christ should come to this same realization. We should update and adjust our belief system to expect earthly resurrections to take place in the present time and not just in the end time.

DELIBERATE RESURRECTIONS

We discussed the fact that Mary and Martha's two particular issues of unbelief tend to personify that of the corporate Church. When the Church begins to update into present truth by rectifying these same issues, resurrections are destined to become more accepted as an integral part of Christian culture. An updated belief system will serve to further reflect that earthly resurrections are not just some incidental and isolated occurrence that happens because God arbitrarily decides to show up.

Earthly resurrections will become deliberate occurrences. Christian believers will have prepared to go about demonstrating the supernatural power of the Holy Spirit in the name of Jesus Christ in this regard. As Christians continue to approach situations of death in deliberate fashion, we can expect an escalation of earthly resurrections in the earth today. The stronghold that death has had on the Body of Christ will gradually begin to be loosened and broken by the authority and dominion of the equipped saints of God in the earth today.

The Church will visibly begin to overcome and prevail over the enemy of death as this escalation continues in the earth.

WE BELIEVE

Let the Church learn to see with different eyes and hear with different ears like Mary and Martha did when it comes to raising the dead. We should move past the mentality where we only believe God to raise someone from a dying bed, and where we stop believing and ministering when someone dies. We can deliberately position ourselves to believe for earthly resurrections after someone dies.

Our thinking and actions of faith should come to reflect the fact that the battle for one's life is not over just because someone dies. To the contrary, ministry could continue.

~

CHAPTER EIGHTEEN

THE DOCTRINES OF CHRIST

*"For since by man came death, by Man also came
the resurrection of the dead."*
1 Corinthians 15:21

The corporate structure of the Church is comprised of several components. The offices of apostles, prophets, evangelists, pastors and teachers are a good example of one component. The nine gifts of the Holy Spirit are also a vital component of the Church. One other component is that of the doctrines of Christ.

Christ's doctrines are listed in Hebrews 6:1-3. The *New King James Version* refers to these particular doctrines as elementary principles. They are listed as:

1) repentance from dead works
2) faith toward God
3) doctrine of baptisms
4) laying on of hands

5) resurrection of the dead
6) eternal judgment

The working realities of these doctrinal truths within the Church were lost during the time of the Dark Ages, generally speaking, between 300 to about 1500 A.D. They were lost on an individual level as well as corporate. They individually began to be restored back into the Church in the 1500s, and consequentially, in corporate fashion. In order to better understand what is implied when using the word *restored*, we will take a historical and very brief overview of the first four doctrines.

We will see that the first four doctrines have already been individually and corporately restored back into the earthly Church in the sequential order in which they are given. The fifth and sixth have not. The restoration of the fifth doctrine, resurrection of the dead, is what this chapter will endeavor to focus upon. In order to more fully comprehend the individual and corporate restoration process of the fifth doctrine, it is helpful to observe the restoration process of the previous four doctrines.

This observation will enable us to better see how Christians raising the dead in the earth today precipitates the restoration of the fifth doctrine — resurrection of the dead.

THE FIRST FOUR DOCTRINES

We are able to observe certain events throughout Church history that affected the corporate disposition of the Church. These various events culminated with the overall restoration of each of Christ's doctrines. Generally speaking, the corporate restoration of the first four doctrines can already be encapsulated throughout certain recognizable time periods in history, whereas the fifth and sixth are yet to be determined.

1) Repentance from dead works   Dark Ages – 1500s
2) Faith toward God   1600s – 1900s
3) Doctrine of baptisms   1900s – 1950s
4) Laying on of hands   1950s – 2000s

An extremely brief overview and highlight of the time period that brought about each doctrine's restoration will be provided. Also noted is the obvious and ever present pattern of opposition and resistance that accompanied these restorations. When we look at the restoration of each doctrine through the eyes of the accompanying resistance, we can get a better feel for what to expect in the way of the fifth doctrine being restored — that is, if we can recognize and accept what is happening to precipitate its restoration.

REPENTANCE FROM DEAD WORKS — DARK AGES - 1500s

We can look back through the eyes of Christian Church history and see that many dead works were taking place during this particular time period. The Church developed into something other than what God intended. It had developed into a religious institution of dead works. Though very real to those practicing these dead works, leaders did not recognize them as dead at the time. Some of these works are as follows.

Forgiveness of sin by private confession to a priest only was one dead work during this time. Today, the corporate Church has the revelation and understanding that Jesus is the High Priest of our confession. Another dead work was a so-called atonement of sins with gifts, good works, self-denial, penance, etc. In reality, it is clearly understood by Christians today that only Jesus can atone for sin. Also, accessing God only through priests or by the authority of the pope was another unnecessary practice of Christians. Today, we can go straight to God for ourselves through the name of Jesus Christ only.

Little by little, Christians began to realize that there was no power in these works. This realization gradually brought about the corporate restoration of Christ's first doctrine, as the second doctrine was now being restored.

FAITH TOWARD GOD — 1500s - 1900s

On October 13, 1517, a man by the name of Martin Luther nailed 95 theses to the door of the Castle Church in Wittenburg, Germany. Luther was basically stating in his theses the many practices and beliefs he deemed unscriptural within the existing Church. He was, in essence, stating that there needed to be repentance from these unscriptural practices and beliefs. Basically, he was trumpeting the second doctrinal truth that man was saved by grace through his faith in God, not through dead and ritualistic works.

Luther's stance was in keeping with the realization of Ephesians 2:8 which states that, *"by grace you have been saved through faith, and that not of yourselves, it is the gift of God."* This truth is very obvious to Christians today, but this was a huge and controversial stand to be taking during that time. Needless to say, Luther stirred up a sea of resistance.

His theses was met with strong resistance and was considered heresy by the religious hierarchy of the day. Other individuals who took up Luther's belief, that individuals are saved by grace through faith in God, were also called heretics and fanatics. The religious hierarchy associated Luther, and other like-minded people, with that of cult status. Needless to say, Luther's revelation of believers being saved by grace through faith, and not by dead works, created a religious revolution.

Approximately one hundred years of religious wars ensued after Luther made his stance known on the door of the Castle Church. The progressive and corporate restoration of this second doctrine climaxed around the 1800s and became more widely accepted. This doctrine remains a fundamental basis of Christianity today within the corporate Church that God is building.

DOCTRINE OF BAPTISMS — 1900s - 1950s

The restorational truths of the third doctrine of Christ were not so readily received within the maturing Church during this time period either. The revelation of this doctrine of *baptisms* also stirred controversy and opposition when it began to be corporately restored. This, of course, depends on what kind of baptism one was referring to — a baptism of repentance, of water, or of the Holy Spirit.

The baptism of repentance is one of turning from sinful ways of life and leaving them behind. The old way of life passes away and all things are made new. Water baptism also became an accepted practice within the Body of Christ during the restoration of this second doctrine. These two baptisms were gradually accepted with relatively little ease compared to the last baptism — the baptism of the Holy Spirit.

The Holy Spirit is the third person of the triune God – the Father, Son and Holy Spirit. When we are baptized in the Holy Spirit we are filled with power and speak with new tongues (Acts 1:4, Acts 1:8 Acts 2:4). Resistance and controversy still follows this baptism to this day primarily because it is associated with speaking in an unknown tongue.

Even though many individuals were reported to have spoken in tongues before the 1900s, the Pentecostal Movement of the early 1900s is noted as a time when this particular baptism began to be corporately birthed in the earth. The great Azusa Street revival, which lasted for three years with thousands in attendance, gave impetus to the corporate restoration of this baptism.

Countless believers received the baptism of the Holy Spirit during this revival. Many still continue to receive this baptism today with evidence of speaking in an unknown tongue, despite the ongoing resistance and controversy of such. Nevertheless, God continued building His Church.

LAYING ON OF HANDS — 1950s-2000

As corporate acceptance of the third doctrine was gaining momentum within the Body of Christ, God continued building His Church by allowing the fourth doctrine, laying of of hands, to begin emerging in corporate fashion. 1 Timothy 4:14, the Apostle Paul told Timothy, "...not to neglect the gift that is in you, which was given to you by prophecy with the laying on of the hands of the eldership [presbytery]." Paul was, in essence, saying that there is an impartation from the Spirit of God that comes with the laying on of hands.

Oral Roberts shocked the vast majority of American audiences when he first began appearing on television during this initial time period. This was because he had the *audacity* to lay his hands on individuals, agreeing and believing that they would receive a miracle. This act was considered a radical practice by not only many religious leaders in the 1950s, but by the secular world as well. Many discounted him for such actions.

In spite of the resistance and controversy over this practice within the Body of Christ, ministers such as T.L. Osborne and Derek Prince, embraced and acted upon this doctrinal practice. Today, it is still a very common practice within present truth churches and ministries. The television exposure of Oral Roberts' ministry swung the door wide open for this doctrinal practice to be revived and restored back into the present day corporate Church like it was in the early Church.

CONTROVERSY AND RESISTANCE

As you can see, one pattern always accompanied the restoration of all four doctrines of Christ as they were being restored. It is the pattern of controversy and resistance. All four doctrines were met with strong opposition as the revelational truths of each of them began to be released to the Body of Christ through various individuals.

No doubt, truths of revelation that are new to us should be spiritually discerned before being accepted. Contemplation and acceptance of such truths during the midst of resistance and controversy takes time. Some individuals never accept and spiritually discern restored truths as revelation from God, while others will continue to progress and act upon the truths being restored.

Nonetheless, each of these four doctrines continues to be progressively integrated within the very fiber and fabric of the Church that God is building today. The restoration of the fifth doctrine should prove to be no exception to this progressive pattern of restoration either. We should remain open to spiritually discern our day of visitation when events begin to unfold in the earth that point to the restoration of the fifth doctrine, resurrection of the dead.

RESURRECTION OF THE DEAD

The vast majority of church historians, major theologians, Christian educators, dispensationalists, etc., generally interpret the restoration of this fifth doctrine as occurring at the point in time when those who have died before us are first resurrected out of their graves. Then, those of us who are alive in Christ Jesus are caught up with them in the air to meet Him in the clouds (1 Thessalonians 4:13-18). In other words, there is a resurrection and then a translation of born-again believers in Jesus Christ.

The author is in agreement with this theology. What has been lacking is the illumination of *how* believers arrive at this end-time translation. In light of the historical pattern of opposition and resistance that accompanied the *progressive* restoration of the first four doctrines of Christ back into the corporate Church, we should at least remain open-minded to recognize and examine how the Body of Christ might possibly progress into the restoration of this fifth doctrine.

With this in mind, the author respectfully submits that an existing and recognizable pattern is progressively coming into focus with regard to the restoration of this fifth doctrine. Some insight into how *this* progressive pattern unfolds is revealed within the Scriptures. The Scriptures reveal an individual and corporate pattern. The unfolding individual pattern is revealed within instances where Jesus raised the dead. The corporate unfolding is revealed as Jesus was being resurrected.

Let's look at the response of what happened when Jesus raised individuals from the dead. Then we will look at what happened in the earth in response to the resurrection power of God at work when Jesus was resurrected.

WHEN JESUS RAISED THE DEAD

We discussed in chapter thirteen, "*...And Many Believed*", what happened when earthly resurrections were demonstrated by Jesus. Consequently, many individuals came to believe on Him throughout whole geographical regions when He raised Jairus' daughter, the widow's son and Lazarus. Based on this biblical pattern we can expect the same result to begin happening in this day and time when Christians deliberately start raising the dead.

This response did not happen just because Jesus was the one raising the dead either. Remember, Peter also encountered and witnessed the same pattern of response after he ministered resurrection life to Dorcas at Joppa. Acts 9:42 states that, "*many believed on the Lord*" after word had spread throughout all of Joppa. This same pattern was evident within certain modern day stories provided in this text. We can expect this same pattern of souls coming to Jesus today as well.

We know that before Jesus comes back that there will be a ripe harvest of souls within the earth (Revelations 14:15-16). We have already established that there is a direct correlation of Christians raising the dead and many souls coming to the Lord when His power is demonstrated in this regard. We can expect that souls coming to believe on Jesus Christ will only continue to increase as more and more Christian believers learn how to demonstrate the resurrection power of the Holy Spirit by raising the dead in the name of Jesus.

The deliberate and frequent occurrence of these earthly resurrections carries the exponential and explosive potential to see that many come to Jesus. A corporate escalation of both Christian believers raising the dead and many coming to the Lord can be expected to occur within the Church. This corporate escalation of an end-time gathering of souls will greatly contribute to the initial preparation for the restoration of the fifth doctrine.

The reality of what happens when this resurrection power operating within the earth peaks into a full-blown corporate move of God can also be observed in Scripture. This insight is revealed within the story of Jesus' personal resurrection and what happened.

WHEN JESUS WAS RESURRECTED

The reverberating and supernatural resurrection power that shook the earth when Jesus was resurrected provides us with some insight as to what we can expect when the corporate escalation of resurrection power peaks within the Body of Christ. This reaction and response to His personal resurrection is accounted for in Matthew 27:50-53.

> [50]"And Jesus cried out again with a loud voice, and yielded up His spirit.
> [51] Then, behold, the veil of the temple was torn in two from top to bottom; and the earth quaked, and the rocks were split,

> ^{52} *and the graves were opened; and many bodies of the saints who had fallen asleep [already died an earthly death] were raised;*
>
> ^{53} *and coming out of the graves after His resurrection, they went into the holy city and appeared to many."*

It should be particularly noted that this resurrection power was so potent that, in addition to the earth quaking and rocks splitting, many other dead saints were affected as well. *"Many bodies of the saints"* that had previously been dead and buried, came up out of their graves. In fact, they appeared to others in the *"holy city"* after Jesus' resurrection took place. Respectfully, this author further submits for consideration that this same corporate pattern can be expected when the end-time resurrection of the saints begins to takes place.

The ongoing resurrecting and escalating power of the Holy Spirit at work today through the equipped saints of God who are raising the dead will eventually trigger this same response. This escalation of power over the enemy of death will culminate at a prevailing degree. It will culminate when all enemies have finally become the footstool of Jesus, especially the enemy of death.

God will once again cause the graves of dead saints to be opened. These believing saints who have been dead will be resurrected and, those of us who are alive at this time, will be translated as we rise to finally meet Jesus in the air. We, too, will appear to others in the *holy city.*

TWO PATTERNS OF PREPARATION

The author is, in essence, submitting two patterns at work in the earth that precipitate the restoration of the fifth doctrine. First, there will be a natural end-time gathering of individuals coming to Jesus Christ as this resurrection power is deliberately imparted and demonstrated by Christian saints raising the dead. Second, as more and more saints receive this spiritual impartation of how to enter into this dimension, and successfully begin raising the dead, this resurrection power will escalate within the earth to a certain degree. It will escalate to a certain degree of overcoming death, that only God knows, and He will cause a supernatural resurrection and translation of the entire Body of Christ — dead and alive.

Again, these two restorational patterns of the fifth doctrine of Christ are submitted for purposes of consideration. The author is unaware of others who have previously submitted these same patterns for consideration. With this in mind, receive them in the light in which they are given.

AGREE TO DISAGREE

Regardless of what we choose to believe about *when* and *how* the restoration of this fifth doctrine unfolds, we can either agree, or agree to disagree. Doctrinal differences should not hinder the ongoing work of the Lord. Meanwhile, Christian believers should make preparation to raise the dead in the earth like Jesus prophetically directed us to do. And further, God's saints will still be resurrected and translated at the end of the earthly Church Age.

The point of focus should remain on the fact that the restoration of the fifth doctrine, resurrection of the dead, will take place in a manner that only the Father knows (Matthew 24:36-44). In the meantime, let's continue to occupy until He comes. The restoration of this doctrine is sure to follow.

ETERNAL JUDGMENT

The author will reserve comment on the sixth and final doctrine, eternal judgment, since the primary focus of this text pertains to resurrection life. The Body of Christ now has ample revelation in front of Her to think about and act upon with regard to the preparation process of the fifth doctrine. In the meantime, let's set our sights on making the enemy of death His footstool so Jesus can return and eternal judgment begin.

THE OVERALL PERSPECTIVE

An overall historical look at Christ's doctrines is just one other perspective through which individuals can easily see that God is building His Church. As we shall see, there are other recognizable events and moves of God throughout Church history whereby we can see that God is building His overcoming and prevailing Church.

CHAPTER NINETEEN

~

I WILL BUILD MY CHURCH

*"And I also say to you that you are Peter, and on
this rock I will build My Church, and the gates of
Hades shall not prevail against it."*
Matthew 16:18

Many believers within the Body of Christ pass through this life
without understanding what, if anything, God is doing in the earth.
A panoramic look at the progressive plan and building process of the
corporate Church is helpful if individuals are going to truly understand
why God desires for believers to raise the dead. In other words,
what on earth has God been doing within the Church and that now
merits the corporate Body of Christ to enter into the dimension of
raising the dead?

It is vital to first have a basic understanding of *how* God is building
and restoring His Church, and *how* this relates to the Body of Christ
today. A glimpse of *how* God has been restoring His Church through
the eyes of Christ's doctrine was discussed in the previous chapter.

Consequently, a small degree of overlapping from that chapter into this chapter will occur. This chapter will approach the building of the Church from an overall perspective of how certain moves of God transpired within the Body of Christ that allowed for certain truths of revelation to be restored.

As we will see, the progressive manner in which God has been building His Church will continue to produce an increased manifestation of the power and demonstration of the Holy Spirit in the earth until Jesus returns.

THE BUILDING PROCESS

Jesus posed a thought provoking question to His disciples in Matthew 16:13-18. The ulterior motive for asking this question was to uniquely unveil and demonstrate how He was going to build His Church, the Body of Christ. His question was this: *"Who do men say that I, the Son of Man, am?"*

Peter, one of His disciples, responded by saying *"You are the Christ, the Son of the living God."* Jesus replied to Peter by saying, *"...flesh and blood has not revealed this to you, but My Father who is in Heaven."* Jesus was, in essence, saying that no human being conveyed this answer to Peter. The answer came by the Spirit of God communicating to the human spirit of Peter.

Jesus goes on to make a far-reaching corporate statement in verse 18. *"And I also say to you that you are Peter, and on this rock* [of revealing] *I will build My church, and the gates of Hades* (Hell) *shall not prevail against it."* We can deduce three things from this Scripture. First, the Church had to be built. And second, it would progressively be built through individuals receiving revelation. Last, when it is finally built the way Jesus intended it to be, the Church will overpower and prevail against the gates of Hell. But first, the Church had to receive the revelation to be able to do this.

The fact that God can speak to all of us means that revelation will always be unfolding and forthcoming. It will come forth for individual purposes, and, it will come forth for the good of the corporate Church as long as the gates of Hell are still prevailing against the Church. Believers within the Body of Christ should keep their spiritual senses exercised to hear what the Holy Spirit is presently revealing to them, whether individually or corporately. The prevailing Church depends upon this fact.

Our concern will be with the corporate revelation God has released, and continues to release, to the Church so that believers will learn how to overpower the enemy of death in the earth.

STAYING UPDATED

The Body of Christ is admonished in 2 Peter 1:12 to *be established in present truth*. This infers that there is a past truth and there is a future truth. Truth is still truth whether it is updated or not, but the Bible admonishes us to be established in present truth. This means that we should be settled and secure in what the Holy Spirit is corporately revealing to believers in the Church that God is building today.

With this in mind, every born-again believer should ask themselves one all important question: In all that God has revealed and restored to the Church throughout the last 2000 years, what is God further revealing and establishing in the way of present truth within the Church today that will cause it to overcome and prevail? Again, a brief overview of the Church's history would be helpful in order to answer this question.

The answer will further help reveal why the Church has now arrived at a place of moving in the power of the Holy Spirit to the degree that believers within the Body of Christ can be expected to raise the dead.

JESUS

The reason we have the Church today is because of Jesus Christ, and none other! Selah! Jesus came, lived and walked upon the earth. His life was an example of how God expects the Body of Christ to live upon this earth. In particular, signs, wonders and miracles followed Him. Sadly enough, so did persecution and ultimate rejection.

According to Matthew 27:50-53, He was physically crucified, spiritually resurrected, physically buried, and then supernaturally rose again. He came back to earth and was seen by man during this time for forty days (Acts 1:2-3). Before He was about to finally ascend to heaven and take His seat at the Right Hand of the Father, He told His apostles to tarry in Jerusalem until the Holy Spirit came.

THE BIRTH AND DIRECTION OF THE CHURCH

The apostles tarried and the Holy Spirit came on the Day of Pentecost, as evidenced with speaking in tongues, and filled them with power. They were now empowered to carry on in the same manner that Jesus demonstrated while He walked upon this earth. Additionally, they would now be prepared to fulfill the Great Commission of Matthew 28:18-20 that Jesus gave them after He rose again, but before He ascended.

He told them in these Scriptures that, [18]*"All authority has been given to me in heaven and on earth.* [19] *Go, therefore, and make disciples of all the nations, baptizing them in the name of the Father, and of the Son, and of the Holy Spirit,* [20] *teaching them to observe all things that I have commanded you; and lo, I am with you always, even to the end of the age."* As the apostles began to *"go"* and adhere to Christ's commands, they were met with the ongoing persecution and resistance to the gospel of Jesus Christ.

A great persecution began to arise against Christians, and they began to scatter for their lives. Through this scattering, the gospel of

Jesus Christ began to spread (Acts 8:1). The persecution and martyrdom of those calling themselves Christians forced many believers to determine just how much they could withstand for being labeled as a follower of Jesus. In other words, many had to be willing to die for taking a Christian stance.

THE DARK AGES

Under the ongoing threat of imminent persecution and martyrdom of Christians well into 300 A.D., the Christian Church (hereinafter referred to as the *"Church"*) slipped into what has aptly been coined the Dark Ages. This was definitely a dark time period in the history of the Church. Corporately speaking, it appeared as if the natural and supernatural realities of the gospel of Jesus Christ had slipped away.

The corporate state of the Church deteriorated and remained in this darkened condition for well over a thousand years. Comparatively speaking, the prevailing Church God said He would build, and the church (hereinafter referred to as *"church"*) that had emerged during this time period, were worlds apart in doctrine and practices. The formal church that had emerged was exercising its authority over man through fear, intimidation and control, not to mention that of practicing dead works. Simply stated, the existing church did not reflect the natural and supernatural ways of Jesus Christ's earthly example to men. As a result, the Church deteriorated into obscurity.

It was not until around the twelfth, thirteenth and fourteenth centuries that devout men like John Wycliffe and John Huss daringly and openly began speaking out about the erroneous teachings and unscriptural practices of what had become the suppressive church. These men declared new and opposing revelation in the face of dire consequences. The most prominent revelation and declaration of truth being made was that Jesus Christ was the head of the Church, and not the pope. Obviously, revelation of this nature went against the grain of the church in that day.

It was vital revelation like this that God was beginning to release to the Body of Christ in order to restore and build the Church His way. Corresponding and similar truths of revelation that men like Wycliff and Huss were declaring gradually began to gain open acceptance and momentum. However, the firm stance taken on these revelational truths did not come without their fair share of resistance, opposition and fatal consequences. Nevertheless, their actions paved the way for more controversial revelation to be ushered into the Church that God was building.

THE PROTESTANT MOVEMENT

On October 31, 1517, a man by the name of Martin Luther continued what Wycliff and Huss had been declaring. He nailed ninety-five theological arguments of the church's unscriptural doctrine's and practices to the Castle Church door in Wittenburg, Germany. These arguments basically stated what was wrong with many of the practices within the church according to the Bible — which, by the way, was now finding its way into the hands of ordinary men and not just the priests. Many historians agree that Luther's overt act earmarked the birth of what is called the Protestant Movement. As a result, a major reformation of the Church was born.

One primary and particular issue Luther zeroed in on was the issue of salvation. The fundamental and commonly accepted belief in the church at this time was that if an individual worked long and hard enough their soul would be saved from hell. In other words, only through good works could one be saved to enter Heaven. Luther's revelation about salvation was obviously in direct opposition to the dominant church's current belief in that day.

Luther protested the church's erroneous belief about salvation by illuminating Ephesians 2:8-9: [8]*"For by grace are ye saved through faith; and that not of yourselves: it is the gift of God: ⁹Not of works, lest any man should boast."* In other words, Luther was stating that we are saved by the grace of God through faith and not by any works we could ever do. In essence, He was *protesting* the predominant belief system of the day with his revelation, especially about salvation.

Luther was eventually ex-communicated from the Roman Catholic Church because he continued to openly declare and stand firm on the ninety-five thesis he nailed to the Castle Church door. There were even serious death threats on his life, but he never backed down from his theological arguments and revelation. Needless to say, the ever-present pattern of opposition and resistance ensued. His radical revelation of *"the just shall live by faith"* ignited a religious revolution that sparked religious wars well into the 1700s.

In spite of the fierce opposition, the corporate belief of salvation being obtained by grace through faith was visibly beginning to settle into the Church God was building. As a result, many Protestant churches were birthed, and Christians were taught *how* to seek and believe God for salvation. Today, many churches only teach about salvation, but God did not stop bringing revelation to the Church after the restorational truth about salvation was illuminated.

As this truth about salvation became embedded into the fabric of the corporate Church, another controversial move of the Holy Spirit began to blow upon the Church in the early 1900s.

THE PENTECOSTAL MOVEMENT

The event that is commonly regarded as the beginning of the Pentecostal Movement in 1900 started in a Bible class in Topeka, Kansas, taught by a man named Charles Parham. Parham specifically challenged his Bible students to study the Scriptures in order to determine the consistent biblical evidence for receiving the gift of the Holy Spirit. When the time came for their answers to be given, they all unanimously determined that the biblical evidence for receiving the gift of the Holy Spirit was speaking in tongues. Consequently, the students ministered among themselves and received this gift according to their biblical findings.

The event that many historians agree earmarked the furtherance of this movement is the well known Azusa Street Revival in Los Angeles, California. It began in 1906 and lasted for three years. This revival catapulted this move of God as thousands of believers came to California from around the world. Many sought, and untold numbers received, the gift of the Holy Spirit in this manner. They, in turn, took this truth of revelation back to their respective nations.

The corporate revelation that was being illuminated to the Church during this movement was similar in nature to that of receiving salvation during the Protestant Movement. Just like individuals of the Protestant Movement could be taught *how* to believe and seek for salvation, now believers could also be taught *how* to believe and seek the baptism of the Holy Spirit. It became corporately apparent in the Church, that receiving the baptism of the Holy Spirit was an experience evidenced with an individual speaking in new tongues, just like on the Day of Pentecost.

Receiving the baptism of the Holy Spirit in this manner is still a vital and integral part of Christianity today. Rather, it should be an integral part of your Christian walk if it is not. According to Acts 2:4, when the Holy Spirit came, it came with the manifestation of tongues. And, Acts 1:8 declares that you shall receive power when the Holy Spirit has come upon you. You will receive this power in order to demonstrate the manner of the kingdom like Jesus did, and do even greater.

The widespread acceptance of this revelation added another building block of power back into the corporate Church. However, God did not stop building the Church with this corporate move of the Spirit either. He further continued building the Church upon the two primary truths of receiving salvation and receiving the baptism of the Holy Spirit.

THE CHARISMATIC MOVEMENT

Another move of the Holy Spirit began to corporately manifest during the 1970s. This move was a continuation of what God started during the Pentecostal Movement. Revelation began to be corporately released with regard to the manifestation of nine gifts that accompany the gift of the Holy Spirit. 1 Corinthians 12:7-11 lists these nine gifts as a word of wisdom, word of knowledge, prophecy, discerning of spirits, different kinds of tongues, interpretation of tongues, gifts of healing, the gift of faith, and the working of miracles.

During this corporate move of God, many teachers began demonstrating and disseminating truths *about* these gifts and what they were. Many teaching materials, in the form of books, workbooks and cassette tapes, were produced on this subject. These teachings were a necessary foundation for preparing the Body of Christ for the next wave of corporate revelation that God would begin revealing and illuminating to the Church.

TRANSITIONING FROM CHARISMATIC TO PROPHETIC

At this point, it is important to be reminded of the fact that unending controversy and resistance accompanied the restoration of salvation being obtained by grace in the Protestant Movement. Controversy and resistance also accompanied the corporate introduction of the baptism of the Holy Spirit with evidence of speaking in tongues during the Pentecostal Movement. What followed the restoration and illumination of the nine gifts of the Holy Spirit during the Charismatic movement would be no exception to this pattern of resistance in the next move of God.

Unlike the challenges of the Protestant and Pentecostal movements which took place long ago, believers of today can move past the restorational truths of previous movements without much of an imminent challenge to their belief system. On the other hand, when we start talking about progressing from the Charismatic movement into the ensuing moves of God, the age-old pattern of opposition and resistance may tend to surface. After all, we are now beginning to deal with individuals of this present time. Belief systems may need to become further updated from restored truths of the past in order to become established in the present truth.

We have already established the truth that believers can teach others *how to* receive salvation. They can also be taught *how to* receive the baptism of the Holy Spirit. Once a person has received the baptism of the Holy Spirit they are endued with power to operate in the gifts of the Holy Spirit, especially the nine gifts that were illuminated during the Charismatic movement. With these restored truths now settled into the corporate Church, it should come as no surprise that the next corporate wave of progressive revelation that God released to the Body of Christ is that individuals can be taught *how to* move and manifest the gifts of the Holy Spirit.

If teaching someone *how to* move in the gifts of the Holy Spirit challenges and sounds foreign to your way of thinking, an update into present truth will be necessary in order to better transition into the next move of God. As in all the prior moves of the Holy Spirit, some make the transition but some simply resist and will not. It is the author's desire for you to be updated as you continue reading.

In order to see this next move of the Holy Spirit adequately accomplished, God saw fit to restore the foundational offices of the prophet and apostle in the 1980s and 1990s, respectively. Believers raised within the more traditional Christian settings may not have been exposed to these two foundational offices. This stands to reason in that they had not yet been restored.

Now that God has restored these offices, an open mind to their acceptance is necessary in order to see more clearly how God continued building His Church.

THE PROPHETIC MOVEMENT

Ephesians 2:20 states that prophets, as well as apostles, comprise the foundation of the Church. This foundational office began to be corporately restored during the 1980s. Amos 3:6 states that *"Surely the Lord God does nothing, unless He reveals His secret to His servants the prophets."* In other words, God reveals and communicates through prophets what He wants trumpeted in the earth. However, prophets should be perceived as more than just a mouthpiece for God in that they only prophesy. Mature prophets are far more than a giver of prophetic words.

In the 1980s, the author was eyewitness to the unfolding of further revelation that God had begun releasing. He was revealing futher expectations of how a prophet should function. Certain prophets began to notice that other observing individuals became capable of prophesying and moving in the gifts of the Holy Spirit alongside of them. Stated another way, prophets were unknowingly imparting the ability to prophesy and move in the gifts of the Holy Spirit to others.

Consequently, a reproducing principle began to emerge within the Body of Christ through this avenue of impartation. One by one, major prophets began to capture this reproducing principle. They established educational settings for imparting and teaching others *how to* manifest and minister their spiritual gifts. As a result, it became apparent and understood that a mature prophet should also be capable of teaching others *how to* prophesy and thereby move in the gifts of the Holy Spirit.

The Apostle Paul had a working knowledge of this principle of impartation as evidenced in Romans 1:11. He told the Christians at

Rome that, *"I long to see you, that I may impart to you some spiritual gift..."*. The restoration of this principle during the prophetic movement began to permeate among the Body of Christ. As a result, thousands were taught, and continue to be taught, *how to* manifest and minister their gifts of the Holy Spirit to this day.

> *Regardless of any and all resistance, God has always continued building His Church.*

This ability to teach others *how to* prophesy and move in the gifts of the Holy Spirit is the major and pivotal distinction to be understood and accepted in order to make the transition from the charismatic movement and into the prophetic movement. For lack of knowledge and understanding about this revelation, believers who have not been predisposed to this type of ministry may at first react by exhibiting the predictable pattern of opposition and resistance. The author's observation and experience is that the resistors of this move of God have the tendency to want to debate and argue that you cannot teach someone *how to* prophesy and move in the gifts of the Holy Spirit.

This tendency is understandable, and grace should be extended to them by those who have already been exposed and established in the working reality of this truth. Regardless of any and all resistance, God has always continued building His Church.

TRANSITIONING FROM THE PROPHETIC TO APOSTOLIC

Although there are many facets of life which merit our attention, it is essential to remain centrally focused on the work of the Holy Spirit. This focus is essential in order to fundamentally understand and properly appropriate the revelation God illuminates to us that will build His Church. The ability to spiritually transition from the prophetic movement and into the apostolic movement is no exception to this statement.

In order to effectively make the fundamental transition from the prophetic into the apostolic, the need exists to take a closer look at what began unfolding during the prophetic movement regarding the manifestation of the nine gifts mentioned in 1 Corinthians 12:7-10. For purposes of this writing, these nine gifts will be broken down into two groups. These two groups will be referred to as the vocal gifts and the power gifts.

The vocal gifts are a *spoken* manifestation of the Spirit of the Lord. They are inclusive of the word of wisdom, word of knowledge, tongues, interpretation of tongues, the gift of prophecy and discerning of spirits. The other three gifts will be referred to as the power gifts: the gift of faith, gift of healing and the working of miracles. As the office of the prophet was being restored, and the gifts of the Holy Spirit were being imparted and reproduced in the 1980s, it became obvious that the vocal gifts were primarily being released and exercised.

This manifestation was understandable given the vocal and audible nature of a prophet's anointing and functioning. On the other hand, the realization began to unfold that the power gifts — gifts that are not necessarily vocal in nature — were lacking in manifestation and expression. The need existed for the power gifts to be imparted and released like vocal gifts had been. It was most befitting that the restoration of the office of apostle — those who are expected to demonstrate the power of God — was on the horizon and coming into focus.

THE APOSTOLIC MOVEMENT

The foundational office of the apostle began to be restored in the 1990s. As we earlier discussed in chapter fifteen, *An Apostolic*

Mandate, one of the expected roles of an apostle is to see the sick healed, lepers cleansed, demons cast out and the dead raised. This expectation is in keeping with what Apostle Paul told the Corinthian church about apostles in 2 Corinthians 12:12. *"Truly the signs of an apostle were accomplished among you with all perseverance, in signs and wonders and mighty deeds."*

Much more could be said about the role and function of apostles. For now, suffice it to say that apostles were being restored and positioned to co-labor with their prophetic counterparts during this time period. The revelation of their role and function was further illuminated to our understanding from New Testament books, such as Matthew and the Acts of the Apostles. Modern day apostles gradually began to realize who they were and what was expected of them in various capacities.

As a result, apostles began to rise in the power and demonstration of the Holy Spirit as their office was being restored. They also began to impart and release their apostolic anointing to others to minister in the power gifts of God as well. In short, God's restoration of this foundational office has triggered a corporate outpouring of the miraculous power of the Holy Spirit in the earth today that will not stop until Jesus comes.

With this in mind, it is of no coincidence that we are seeing the supernatural manifestation of the miraculous power of the Holy Spirit being released in the earth today throughout the Body of Christ. This outpouring will only increase as God's Kingdom continues to manifest in the earth. His power will manifests to the degree that all enemies, including the enemy of death, becomes His footstool by the equipped saints of God within the Body of Christ.

THE SAINTS MOVEMENT

Apostles and prophets were restored in order to see that the saints of God became more fully equipped, supernaturally as well as naturally, according to Ephesians 4:11-12. Again, these two verses state that, [11] "*...He Himself gave some to be apostles, some prophets, some evangelists, and some pastors and teachers,* [12] *for the equipping of the saints for the work of ministry, for the edifying of the body of Christ.*"

It is interesting to reflect back in time when the visible restoration of these five governmental offices began to take place. Take note of what happened on May 14, 1948. As a fulfillment of biblical prophecy, Israel became a self-governing state for the first time in over two thousand years. A corporate move of God to restore these five offices began to take place after this momentous event. They visibly began to be restored at an accelerated pace compared to other restorational moves of God.

The office of an evangelist, as well represented by Oral Roberts and T.L. Osborne, was restored to the Church in the 1950s. The 1960s brought about the restoration of the pastoral office. Kenneth Hagin, Fred Price and Kenneth Copeland are primary ministers who paved the way for the restoration of the office of the teacher in the 1970s. When you mention the restoration of the office of prophet during the 1980s, the most prominent and pioneering name that comes to mind is Bill Hamon. John Eckhardt stands out among those whom God used in the 1990s to help restore the office of the apostle.

This time line now brings us to the 21st Century. All five-fold offices have been restored. The saints have been equipped to move in the power and demonstration of the Holy Spirit. This restoration and equipping of the saints has resulted in what is now being called the *Saints Movement*.

The Saints Movement will see the everyday believer, like Stephen (Acts 6:8) and Philip (Acts 8:5-8), begin demonstrating the power of God like five-fold ministry leaders within the Church should be doing. These believing saints will not be limited and confined to operate in the power of the Holy Spirit only within the four walls of the Church.

They will demonstrate everywhere they go, seven days a week, because they are spiritually equipped to do so.

The equipped saints of God will influence and impact schools, communities, businesses, corporations and governments. Whether through a word of knowledge about a business strategy, the ministry of healing to the head of a corporation, or a word of wisdom about policy making, this is the power of the Holy Spirit at work in the Body of Christ today. As a result, cities, states and nations will be directly affected as the Church continues to transition out of its inward-looking posture and into the world during this movement.

INCREASE OF POWER

When the Church is finally built the way God intends it be, it will be a Church that knows how to overcome and prevail over *all* the enemies of Jesus and make them His footstool. God meant it when He said He would build His Church and the gates of Hades shall not prevail against it. Before this could happen, the overcoming and prevailing power of the Holy Spirit had to be restored back into the Church.

This increase of the Holy Spirit's miraculous power will only continue to escalate well into the 21st Century. This escalation points to what will ultimately lie ahead for the Body of Christ when God has fully restored and finished building His earthly Church. It will culminate with the ultimate return of Jesus Christ.

Let the Church continue to arise in the power and demonstration of the Holy Spirit in all aspects of society until God, through the Body of Christ, prevails in making all of Jesus Christ's enemies His footstool.

CHAPTER TWENTY

~

THE RESTORATION OF
ALL THINGS

[19]"Repent therefore and be converted, that your sins may be blotted out, so that times of refreshing may come from the presence of the Lord, [20] and that He may send Jesus Christ, who was preached to you before, [21] whom heaven must receive until the times of restoration of all things, which God has spoken by the mouth of all His holy prophets since the world began."

Acts 3:19-22

As we can see from the above referenced verses, Jesus must be held in the heavens until *the restoration of all things, which God has spoken by the mouth of all His holy prophets since the world began.* The Bible speaks of the restoration of the Church, Israel and the earth. The focus of this text has obviously been on the restoration of the Church.

The Church's restoration has visibly been in process since the 1500s. This overall process has not come without it fair share of resistance and opposition. And, the battle is not over yet. It will be over when, first and foremost, the Church is fully restored and ready for Jesus. All enemies will have been made the footstool of Jesus.

Satan will attempt to throw us his best shots of opposition and resistance in order to keep this restoration from happening. As in any type of battle, the fighting is the fiercest at the end when it looks as if one or the other is about to go down. Since the message of this book is directly tied to overcoming this last enemy of the earthly Church, the battle only heats up once we begin acting upon the truths of this message. It will literally be a fight to the resurrection.

Despite any and all opposition, the Church is destined to arise in power and demonstration greater than that of the early Church. It will have to arise in this manner in order to prevail over the enemy of death in the earth. The most Holy Prophet of all, Jesus, has declared it to be so.

RESTORATION

Strong's Concordance states that the word "restoration" used in Acts 3:21 is the Greek word "apokatastasis" (ap-ok-at-as-tas-is). This word means "restitution." If you have ever had to make restitution for something, you have either had to pay or give something back, in order to make up for damage or a loss. This is so the damage can be repaired and returned to its earlier state in order to become better than it was originally.

In order to see how today's restored Church will be better supernaturally than it was in its earlier state, a look at its earlier state in this regard is necessary.

The Church was birthed on the Day of Pentecost. Its earlier state was when the apostles, prophets and saints walked the earth demonstrating the supernatural power of the Holy Spirit like Jesus did. The sick were healed, withered hands recreated, demons were cast out, food was multiplied, the dead were raised, not to mention the manifestation of other kinds of supernatural miracles. In other words, it was natural for the supernatural to manifest in the early Church.

The supernatural ability of the Church in this day and time will have to be restored in order to see Acts 3:19-21 fulfilled. But, just like a piece of furniture gets stripped of everything but the raw wood before it can be fully restored, so it is with the Church. The Church was virtually stripped of everything but the Apostle's Creed. In the 1500s, we slowly began to see a return to the Church's earlier state when God began restoring and re-establishing doctrinal truths to the Body of Christ.

Today, the proper infrastructure continues to be restored and set into place. The working realities of Christ's doctrines, the five-fold governmental offices, and especially, the supernatural power of the Holy Spirit, continues to be corporately re-established within the Church. Once the Church is restored like God intends to be, it will be greater in power and demonstration than the earlier Christian Church. But remember, we still have a raging battle in front of us to confront.

OPPOSITION AND RESISTANCE

We should not think that our adversary, the devil, is idly sitting by and watching this restoration and transformation of the Church take place. The time that he has left here on this earth is prolonged by the inability of the Church to prevail over all Her enemies. Stated another way, as long as the devil can prevent the Church from being fully restored to the point that She cannot prevail over all Her enemies, and make them the footstool of Jesus, then the devil and his cohorts are free to continue roaming this earth through other human beings — stealing, killing and destroying (John 10:10).

As long as the devil can find individuals who are willing to cooperate with him, whether knowingly or unknowingly, he will continue to roam the earth in this manner. His purpose is to stop the restoration of the Church, as well as Israel and the earth, through whatever means he can. Christian believers raising the dead, in particular, will certainly be no exception to his centuries-old strategy of opposition and resistance. Prevailing over death is the biggest threat to his demise on planet earth.

As long as he can keep the message of this book from being accepted, practiced and successfully demonstrated, he will. The good news is that he cannot. The not-so-welcome news is that his opposition and resistance is sure to surface with a fierce vengeance from all directions against the saints of God willing to come against the enemy of death. It is for this reason that this author, as a prophetess of God, prophetically declares that the equipped saints of God are being prepared to enter into an inevitable and headlong battle with the devil in order to overcome and prevail over this enemy of death.

Our human opposers that the devil and his cohorts work through will think that it is outright illogical, unfathomable, unthinkable, unattainable and utterly unfounded that Christian believers can be instrumental in raising a dead person. It will simply be in-comprehensible to their way of thinking and believing. Like Jesus, we may very well be mocked and scoffed at by them in general, and especially, when we enter into these situations. To say the least, we will have a major learning curve to endure and survive as we encounter opposition and resistance in this regard.

The ingrained design of such opposition and resistance to God's progressive plan and purposes for the Church's restoration is to cause the equipped saints of God to draw back. For instance, when it looks as if the first few deceased individuals we minister to do not raise like we thought, are we going to back down? When we have to experience the not-so-pleasant emotional let-down of family members whose loved one was not raised, will we stand to minister again? Or, are we going to continue pressing in to the Spirit of God and say that "we are indeed able" to overcome this seemingly formidable giant in the land?

I earlier provided you with the factual information (in chapter fifteen, *An Apostolic Mandate*) that over 300 individuals had been raised from the dead within the scope of David Hogan's ministry. It is only fair and balanced for you to also know that, in light of the 300 deceased who were raised, he also stated that over 1,000 deceased had received ministry to be raised. From the opposite perspective, a little over seven hundred deceased individuals did not come back to life that had received ministry.

This ministry did not quit and back down just because the majority was not being raised. The good news is that a few hundred resurrected people came back to life to be with their living loved ones. A conscious choice was made to continue ministering resurrection life despite the odds. Resurrection life still continues to be ministered by this prototypical ministry today, and the numbers are climbing.

Those of us responsible to raise the dead, and desiring to raise the dead, should let this observation be an invaluable lesson of insight upon entering into this dimension. Our work will be cut out for us as we incorporate this dimension of faith into our journey in order to successfully prevail upon this enemy of death. We will have our share of disappointments and times of discouragement. However, we cannot let these times cause us to draw back. If anything, we should let these experiences serve to cause us to press in.

Pressing in may be easier said than done, but in reality, the only way we are going to overcome this enemy is by continuing to press in to this dimension in spite of our human shortcomings.

THE ENEMIES OF SICKNESS AND DISEASE

The fact that the focus of this book is centered on the enemy of death should not be construed to mean that death is the only enemy to overcome. Granted, there are other enemies, but the enemy of death has been the least apprehended by the Body of Christ. This subject definitely deserves our attention for this and one other important reason.

Further revelation for overcoming sickness and disease can be ascertained in light of revelation of how to minister resurrection life. Generally speaking, when we take a step back and *see* with spiritual eyes how to overcome death, new insight can be illuminated to our understanding on how to overcome the enemies of sickness and disease. Take special note of the following in order to see what is meant by these two preceding statements.

When Christian believers start seeing the necessary actions of faith required to successfully raise the dead, we will begin to see more clearly what it takes for healing, deliverance, and other miracles to come forth. For instance, when resurrection life is successfully ministered to a deceased, it is because the individuals ministering continued with their ongoing actions of faith by staying until the deceased was raised. The key here is that the ministers had faith to believe that the deceased was going to be raised and, as evidenced by their persevering actions, they were not leaving until the resurrection came to pass.

A prime example of this fact is found in an extraordinary, miraculous story, where the author who repeats it went to great lengths to insure its authenticity. It is the story about a young Christian woman who had a baby in a remote tribal village of India. And I quote: *"It was not a happy event. It was a tragedy."*

> *"The baby had two heads. It was not even a Siamese-twin type of problem, but a case where a second head was growing out of the top of the first. Also, it had only one real eye; the other three*

places that ought to have been eyes were just lumps of flesh... They felt they should just put the thing in a clay pot and throw it out into the jungle for the animals to eat... But finally they decided, 'No, we're Christians now, so we shouldn't do that. We should pray for this baby.'"

"*As they poured their hearts out in intercessory prayer, the Lord was moved, and the girl's face began to change. They prayed all night, and by morning, she was a beautiful infant girl, normal in every way, with one head and two normal eyes!*"[1] The point to be emphasized here is that these Christians gathered together and did not quit their ministry until the baby was healed.

The Body of Christ will be impressed upon to act on this same principle when sickness, disease and other enemies threaten, whether the consequences are dire or not. Individuals will need to come forth with the same kind of enduring faith in order to minister in this committed manner until the desired results are achieved. These individuals, or even a rotating team, will stay until the person is free from their sickness or disease.

This type of ministry will take individuals willing to give of their time and commit to these situations. It will also give added meaning to "going to pray for" someone.

THE DICTATES OF WISDOM

The revelation for going on the offense against the enemy of death has, in general, been upheld from the eyes of our corporate understanding. Now that God is corporately releasing and illuminating this type of revelation, it is up to the Body of Christ to **wisely**

---

1. Rutz, James, *Megashift, Igniting Spiritual Power*, Empowerment Press, Colorado Springs, Colorado, 2005, pp. 108-9.

disseminate and *wisely* act upon its truths. Else, if we do not, we will run the risk of making the same and re-occurring mistakes of the prior moves of God. We will swing to the extreme and generate unnecessary misunderstandings, confusion and spiritual chaos. Why run the risk if we can minimize it with wisdom and counsel?!

This is one move of God we do not want to jeopardize in this manner if we can avoid it. This risk can be somewhat minimized and tempered by first submitting ourselves to counsel before acting in these situations, when possible. This is not to say that hurtful mistakes will not be made. Mistakes will be made, but they do not have to be made in an unnecessary or zealous manner.

The devil is already going to do what he can to prevent us from raising the dead. For this reason alone, we would be wise to surround and fortify ourselves with others of like mind when it comes to ministering resurrection life.

TEAM MINISTRY

We should remember that we do not have biblical account where Jesus ministered resurrection life to deceased individuals alone. He was involved in situations where His disciples were with Him, or, where He knew the individuals to whom He was ministering. In light of Jesus' example, team ministry should become even more important to recognize and emphasize in this next move of God.

Team ministry, where resurrection life is concerned, will be helpful in a number of ways. One, it will help provide for some much needed wisdom and counsel in making crucial decisions that these complex and varying situations of death can elicit during the process. This is not to say that we will not ever find ourselves ministering alone, such as in auto accidents, etc. But, when we can avoid ministering alone, we should.

Another advantage of team ministry is realized when the ministry becomes prolonged. If you will remember, there will be those instances where the deceased is not immediately raised. When this is the case, other committed individuals can come on the scene and rotate in shifts so the ministry to the deceased can continue.

Other advantages to team ministry will be forthcoming. The advantage for ongoing counsel and extended ministry are just two prime reasons why we would be well advised to strongly consider the team ministry approach when ministering resurrection life. Proverbs 24:6 states, *"For by wise counsel you will wage your own war, And in a multitude of counselors there is safety."*

THE PREVAILING CHURCH

God said in Matthew 16:18 that He would build His Church to the degree that the gates of Hades of would not prevail against it. The word "prevail" in the Greek language is "katischuo". It literally means to "overpower." If anything, the Church has been overpowered by Her enemies for centuries. This pattern is reversing as the Church is being restored. Instead, the Church prevails against the gates of Hell through the power and demonstration of the Holy Spirit. Specifically speaking, it will prevail against the enemy of death!

It is interesting to consider various implications to society as the Church begins to prevail over the enemy of death. For example, it will have implications in areas such as the insurance industry, funeral home business, and in hospitals and hospices. These implications become rather obvious when you think through a situation where someone is resurrected.

Raising the dead will have legal implications to insurance companies, especially in terms of payouts. For instance, will a life insurance company pay a death benefit to someone who was verifiably and legally dead, and then is subsequently resurrected? After all, these payouts are *death benefits*. A decision will have to be made when a notarized and valid death certificate is presented, especially from the person who was resurrected.

231

Insurance companies will have to go back to the drawing board on this one. A good recommendation to start out with is that they reconsider their use of what they attribute to their policy language, "acts of God". In doing so, they may want to first take a look at John 10:10 for some insight into this suggestion. *"The thief does not come except to steal, and to kill, and to destroy. I [Jesus] have come that they may have life, and that they may have it more abundantly."*

Raising the dead is a life giving act of God. Hurricanes, earthquakes, and so forth, are acts of the devil. They steal, kill and destroy life. The devil came and brought sin into the earth that, when left to run its course, it would ultimately lead to stealing, killing and destroying on all levels. These corporate catastrophes are in response to corporate sin running rampant in the earth, or should I say the absence of God in our lives.

When we vote and tell God to get out of our personal lifestyles, educational systems, businesses, and governments, He will. And we are seeing the result of His absence through these catastrophes in the earth today. God says in 2 Chronicles 7:14-15, *"...if My people who are called by My name will humble themselves, and pray and seek My face, and turn from their wicked ways, then I will hear from heaven, and will forgive their sin and* **heal their land***.*

Let's give credit to where credit is due, but let's not attribute these catastrophes to God just because we think He could have prevented them. Let's open our eyes to the reality that there is a real devil out there *"seeking whom he may devour."* According to *1 Peter 5:8* we should *"Be sober, be vigilant; because your adversary the devil walks about like a roaring lion, seeking whom he may devour."* These devouring acts are "acts of the devil" that should be attributed to him, and not God.

Insurance companies are not the only ones to be affected by Christians raising the dead. Funeral homes will also be affected.

Funeral homes are called funeral homes because that's what they are in the business of conducting — a funeral. On the other hand, we could find these businesses expanding their services and evolving to accommodate living loved ones in a different way. The use of their facilities could evolve into a place where resurrection ministry is permissible.

As you can imagine, hospitals and hospices could very well be affected as well when someone dies. Re-consideration of options and procedures for the removal, examination and riddance of a corpse are a real possibility. On another note, these institutions could end up changing the job description of their chaplains and emergency personnel and allow for resurrection life to be ministered.

These are just a few ways in which the successful ministry of Christians raising the dead will potentially affect society. Others are bound to surface as the equipped and empowered believers of the Saints Movement wisely, but unashamedly, step forward to minister in the power and demonstration of the Holy Spirit.

THE LAST DAYS CHURCH

The Old Testament prophet, Joel, gave a prophecy of some things that would come to pass in the "last days" (Joel 2:28-29). This same prophesy is reiterated in the New Testament by Peter in Acts 2:16-18. The following is what Joel prophesied:

> [28]"And it shall come to pass in the last days, says God, that I will pour out My Spirit on all flesh; Your sons and your daughters shall prophesy, Your old men shall dream dreams, Your young men shall see visions.
> [29] And also on My menservants and on My maidservants I will pour out My Spirit in those days. And they shall prophesy."

God is not dribbling out His Spirit to us in these last days. He is *pouring* out His Spirit in response to the Body of Christ's ability to manifest their spiritual gifts. In the process, we will begin to hear people talk about a dream from God that they had. It will become common for someone to say "I had a vision". And do not be surprised if your son or daughter tells you that they prophesy. These things coming to pass are a literal fulfillment of prophecy from the prophet, Joel.

Prophet Joel was not the only one to prophesy concerning the latter Church. The prophet Haggai did too, in Haggai 2:6-9.

> ⁶ "... I will shake heaven and earth, the sea and dry land;
>
> ⁷ 'and I will shake all nations, and they shall come to the Desire of All Nations, and I will fill this temple with glory,' says the LORD of hosts.
>
> ⁸ 'The silver is Mine, and the gold is Mine,' says the LORD of hosts.
>
> ⁹ 'The glory of this latter temple shall be greater than the former,' says the LORD of hosts."

It would be easy to become sidetracked with the scope of this prophetic word today in that it pertains to the earth, sea, land and nations being shaken. Needless to say, there is a whole lot of shaking going on but there is much more shaking to be done.

The *"shaking"* that is spoken of in this Scripture points to the end-time prophetic fulfillment of what would ultimately happen in the earth, sea and dry land that would affect the latter-day Church. The latter-day Church will be affected by this *"shaking."* The ongoing shaking will eventually cause nations to turn to Jesus Christ, *"the Desire of All Nations."*

Haggai went on to prophetically declare how the Church will be in the last days. He stated that the glory of this latter day temple would be greater than the glory of the former temple. The Old Testament Hebrew word for "glory" is the word "kabod." It is from the root word "kabed" (*Strong's Concordance*). The word "kabed" has several different words given to its meaning. Oddly enough, one of these words is none other than the word "prevail!"

With this definition in mind, we can then interpret this verse to mean that, the prevailing of the latter day Church will be greater than the prevailing of the former Church.

BREAKING THE APPOINTMENT WITH DEATH

Everything that Jesus and the early Church did to prevail upon our enemies will be prevailed upon even greater in the latter Church that God is restoring. The latter Church will have to be greater than the former day Church for at least one good reason. The latter Church will at some point have to break death's appointment in the earth.

Psalms 102:19-20 states,

> [19] "*For He looked down from the height of His sanctuary; From heaven the LORD viewed the earth,*
> [20] *To hear the groaning of the prisoner, To release those appointed to death.*"

This last verse means that there is a generation to come that will be released from seeing death in the earth. These are the saints who will be caught up to be with Jesus, after the dead in Christ rise first, when He comes back for the Church (1 Thessalonians 4:17).

In essence, there has to be a generation that will come forth in resurrection power to the degree that they will break their appointment with death in the earth. They will fulfill the restorational process of the Church by bringing the Body of Christ to a place where She prevails over this last enemy. This is the generation of the Church to whom God corporately releases the necessary revelation for how to begin overcoming death in the earth.

In light of the above, the author respectfully submits that the generation of equipped saints who rise in resurrection power and break this appointment with death is alive. They will carry the message of this text to the end of the earthly Church Age.

PROPHETIC UNDERSTANDING

When we understand the overall picture of how God has been building and restoring His Church throughout history, we can prophetically understand why God is bringing the Church to a place where He expects the Body of Christ to begin prevailing upon the enemy of death. The resurrection power of the Holy Spirit over death has to first be restored to the earthly Church in order for the Body of Christ to be resurrected and meet Jesus in the air.

Let resurrection life wisely begin to be ministered by the equipped saints of God amid the forces of unbelief as the Church advances into this next supernatural dimension! In the process, it will become as natural for the equipped saints of God to begin manifesting the supernatural power of the Holy Spirit in the restored Church as it is for us to take our next breath. This supernatural increase of power and demonstration will cause the principles of the Kingdom of God to become established in the earth like never before.

Let God's kingdom continue to come, and His will be done on earth, as it is in heaven, *until the restoration of all things*. And, *"the kingdoms of this world have become the kingdom of our Lord" (Revelation 11:15)*.

Chapter Twenty-One

~

Conclusion

An individual and corporate perspective of Christians raising the dead has been presented. This text, however, should in no way be construed as an exhaustive work. It is but a fundamental and basic presentation in that the subject itself needs to be resurrected. This text only begins to scratch the surface. The message of it, however, is one that will once again visibly revolutionize and shape the face of the ever-maturing Church.

The study of past, present and future resurrection miracles will yield deeper revelation and further unfold biblical insights yet to be unearthed. As a result, many more books on this subject will be forthcoming in days ahead that will render invaluable and educational insights. As for this particular presentation, hopefully it has served the basic purpose of inciting you to consider making preparation to enter into this dimension.

I should reiterate that the insights and morsels of wisdom of this text *should not* be perceived, received and construed as some sort of tried and proven formula or methodology. Faith is not predicated upon formulas or methodology, but upon faith in a relationship with the Lord, Jesus Christ. Rather, these insights and morsels of wisdom should serve the purpose of revealing the probability and permissibility of unconventional behaviors of faith that may at times be associated with just getting into these situations, not to mention ministering resurrection life.

Our actions of faith are to be borne and birthed out of our spirit while walking out one of these particular situations, and not out of some text. The stories within this text present only a miniscule few of the many unconventional actions that faith-filled men and women of God had to take in order to overcome the premature grips of death on a person. The unbelief and resistance encountered in walking out their decision to enter into this dimension should serve as an example of what we could possibly expect in our own personal encounters.

To say the least, entering into this dimension on a literal basis will be a maturing process for us all. This will be especially true starting out. We will have to learn how to move past disappointing and discouraging situations of death where deceased were not raised, and leave the situations in God hands. This will be necessary in order to rise to the occasion the next time we find ourselves confronted with death. And, we should determine that there will be a next time.

On a more positive note, it should be noted that with experience comes maturity. While the initial level of maturity of this dimension may understandably be lacking, it certainly is not what it is going to be in the future. It is for this reason that training and equipping the saints of God to enter into these situations should be a priority. This training and equipping will take some time and hands on experiences.

Given this fact, Jesus is probably not coming back as *soon* as we would like to think. We may be living in the *last days*, but the *last-days* Church will have to see a generation that is trained, equipped and prevailing over the enemy of death. Individually speaking, do you see or hear of the dead being raised around you? Corporately speaking, do you see or hear of the dead frequently being raised in the global Church? If not, God is probably not coming back as soon as we would like to think.

This period of time we call *soon* hinges upon responsible people taking their rightful place within the Body of Christ. There is still plenty of teaching and demonstration to be done in the Church concerning this dimension alone before Jesus can return. Jesus is coming back for a mature Church — a Church that is quite capable of overcoming death. If we want the Lord to come back soon, then we should do what we can in order to see that this message becomes established within the Church.

If the contents of this book are far removed from your beliefs and ways of thinking, re-consider your beliefs. Specifically, take a look at your life in relation to Jesus Christ in order to better ascertain the many benefits of being born again. If you have not been born-again in Jesus Christ, according to John 3:16, there has never a better time to stop and ask the Lord, Jesus Christ to come into your heart as your personal Savior.

If you have asked the Lord Jesus Christ to come into your heart as your personal Savior, and the contents of this book are still somewhat removed from your comprehension, then an update into present truth may very well be in order. You may have some conscious decisions to make about your spiritual, not religious, life. A major change may be in order to realize that there are many more spiritual benefits to salvation than just missing eternal hell.

Those of you who are born again and already operating in the power of the Holy Spirit, and can identify with the contents of this book, prepare yourselves for this move of God. Apostles and prophets, assume your rightful place and lead the way. Start making a concerted and deliberate effort to prepare yourselves and others to raise the dead.

Our first personal goal should be to see that those close to us become educated about this subject. This includes those who are responsible for us upon our death, or, those to whom we are responsible for upon their death. See that other individuals within your sphere of influence are exposed to this message. And remember, we owe it to the following generation to see that they are equipped to act on this message.

This subject of Christians raising the dead has been discussed in our home over and over since my son, Drew, was ten years of age. His mentality (when he is not playing tennis or watching University of Georgia football) is that Christians raising the dead is an integral part of Christianity. Right after Drew turned 13, I unassumingly asked him one day if he thought he would raise the dead. Without hesitation, he responded by saying, "Sure, one day."

The point being made here is that raising the dead is not an insurmountable issue within my son's thinking. He has been involuntarily subjected and educated to what the Word of God has to say on this issue from a young age. Likewise, responsible believers within the Body of Christ should ensure that the younger generation is wisely handed the spiritual mentality that raising the dead is a very realistic possibility. After all, they are the generation responsible for seeing that this restorational move of God is fully ushered into the earth to such degree that Jesus can return.

Jesus longs to return and be reunited with us just as much as we long to be united with Him. He has waited over 2,000 earth years for the Body of Christ to mature into Her own spiritual strength and power in order to overcome all our enemies. Luke 10:19 tells us that, *"Behold, I give you the authority…over all the power of the enemy, and nothing shall by any means hurt you."* Let the Church come forth in this authority and power in order to begin prevailing over this last enemy of death in the earth.

The sooner we begin prevailing, the sooner we will be resurrected and translated into immortality. *"So when this corruptible has put on incorruption, and this mortal has put on immortality, then shall be brought to pass the saying that is written: "Death is swallowed up in victory"* (1 Corinthians 15:54-55). Then, the resurrected Body of Christ can wholeheartedly echo with a united and orchestrated voice and say, *"O death where is thy victory? O Hades, where is thy sting?"*(1 Corinthians 15:54-55).

Our faith in Jesus Christ, our Lord and Savior, will have truly made us whole!

Author's Comments

My heart's desire through this book has been to embolden saints to set their ultimate sights on seeing that the earthly Church's enemy of death is overcome. The Body of Christ has only scratched the surface of this dimension. There is much more revelation and information to be revealed. Along this same line, I hope you will consider sharing authenticated, resurrection stories with me as I endeavor to fulfill the vision and goal God has given.

God said to, *"Write the vision and make it plain on tablets, that he may run who reads it. For the vision is yet for an appointed time; but at the end it will speak, and it will not lie. Though it tarries, wait for it; because it will surely come. It will not tarry"* (Habakkuk 2:2-3).

VISION

1. To be a resource center for Christians desiring to raise the dead, with the Holy Bible being our foremost resource. To gather authentic, resurrection stories for careful study, assimilation and documentation for the very educational and spiritual purposes they will yield to the Body of Christ.

2. To facilitate the restoration of this resurrection miracle by imparting this message to other Christian believers. To help teach and train Christian believers to become better equipped and empowered, through various educational venues, in order to overcome the enemy of death.

3. To become a catalyst for assisting individuals who find themselves confronted with death situations.

4. To track the Church's corporate progress and advancement over the enemy of death throughout various geographical regions.

GOAL

To make the ministry of raising the dead as common as the ministry of healing the sick, cleansing the lepers and casting out demons.

YOUR SUPPORT

It is for the stated vision and goal that I invite you to consider supporting this ministry with your tax-deductible donations. The vision has been written and made plain. Please consider becoming a part of what God is restoring to the Church today by financially sowing into this ministry at:

Diane S. Morrison
Morrison Ministries, Inc.
P.O. Box 6400
Destin, Florida 32550
USA

May the blessing of what you sow truly be yours in the successful reaping of this message to other deceased individuals.

CHURCH! COME FORTH
TEACHING AND TRAINING

Have you prepared to raise the dead?

The "Church! Come Forth" teaching is an educational training tool that will advance believers in the Body of Christ to another level of faith for raising the dead. Discover how born again believers in Jesus Christ can wisely and insightfully approach situations of death. The knowledge and revelation for raising the dead should be instilled within our spirits long before any of us are ever faced with a situation of premature death.

Faith for raising the dead will come by hearing what the Word of God has to say on this subject *NOW*. In other words, now is the time to prepare to raise the dead, not when someone dies.

This teaching will help...
- *Reveal another level of faith in God!*
- *Spiritually prepare and equip you to raise the dead!*
- *Build confidence and boldness within you to approach deceased individuals!*

The concept and working reality of Christians raising the dead back to earthly life will once again be restored as an integral part of our Christian culture, just as it was in the early Church.

For further information or ministry scheduling please go to:
www.churchcomeforth.com